C-4869   CAREER EXAMINATION SERIES

This is your
PASSBOOK for...

Elevator & Escalator Specialist

Test Preparation Study Guide
Questions & Answers

NATIONAL LEARNING CORPORATION®

COPYRIGHT NOTICE

This book is SOLELY intended for, is sold ONLY to, and its use is RESTRICTED to individual, bona fide applicants or candidates who qualify by virtue of having seriously filed applications for appropriate license, certificate, professional and/or promotional advancement, higher school matriculation, scholarship, or other legitimate requirements of education and/or governmental authorities.

This book is NOT intended for use, class instruction, tutoring, training, duplication, copying, reprinting, excerption, or adaptation, etc., by:

1) Other publishers
2) Proprietors and/or Instructors of "Coaching" and/or Preparatory Courses
3) Personnel and/or Training Divisions of commercial, industrial, and governmental organizations
4) Schools, colleges, or universities and/or their departments and staffs, including teachers and other personnel
5) Testing Agencies or Bureaus
6) Study groups which seek by the purchase of a single volume to copy and/or duplicate and/or adapt this material for use by the group as a whole without having purchased individual volumes for each of the members of the group
7) Et al.

Such persons would be in violation of appropriate Federal and State statutes.

PROVISION OF LICENSING AGREEMENTS – Recognized educational, commercial, industrial, and governmental institutions and organizations, and others legitimately engaged in educational pursuits, including training, testing, and measurement activities, may address request for a licensing agreement to the copyright owners, who will determine whether, and under what conditions, including fees and charges, the materials in this book may be used them. In other words, a licensing facility exists for the legitimate use of the material in this book on other than an individual basis. However, it is asseverated and affirmed here that the material in this book CANNOT be used without the receipt of the express permission of such a licensing agreement from the Publishers. Inquiries re licensing should be addressed to the company, attention rights and permissions department.

All rights reserved, including the right of reproduction in whole or in part, in any form or by any means, electronic or mechanical, including photocopying, recording, or by any information storage and retrieval system, without permission in writing from the Publisher.

Copyright © 2024 by
National Learning Corporation

212 Michael Drive, Syosset, NY 11791
(516) 921-8888 • www.passbooks.com
E-mail: info@passbooks.com

PUBLISHED IN THE UNITED STATES OF AMERICA

PASSBOOK® SERIES

THE *PASSBOOK® SERIES* has been created to prepare applicants and candidates for the ultimate academic battlefield – the examination room.

At some time in our lives, each and every one of us may be required to take an examination – for validation, matriculation, admission, qualification, registration, certification, or licensure.

Based on the assumption that every applicant or candidate has met the basic formal educational standards, has taken the required number of courses, and read the necessary texts, the *PASSBOOK® SERIES* furnishes the one special preparation which may assure passing with confidence, instead of failing with insecurity. Examination questions – together with answers – are furnished as the basic vehicle for study so that the mysteries of the examination and its compounding difficulties may be eliminated or diminished by a sure method.

This book is meant to help you pass your examination provided that you qualify and are serious in your objective.

The entire field is reviewed through the huge store of content information which is succinctly presented through a provocative and challenging approach – the question-and-answer method.

A climate of success is established by furnishing the correct answers at the end of each test.

You soon learn to recognize types of questions, forms of questions, and patterns of questioning. You may even begin to anticipate expected outcomes.

You perceive that many questions are repeated or adapted so that you can gain acute insights, which may enable you to score many sure points.

You learn how to confront new questions, or types of questions, and to attack them confidently and work out the correct answers.

You note objectives and emphases, and recognize pitfalls and dangers, so that you may make positive educational adjustments.

Moreover, you are kept fully informed in relation to new concepts, methods, practices, and directions in the field.

You discover that you are actually taking the examination all the time: you are preparing for the examination by "taking" an examination, not by reading extraneous and/or supererogatory textbooks.

In short, this PASSBOOK®, used directedly, should be an important factor in helping you to pass your test.

ELEVATOR AND ESCALATOR SPECIALIST

DUTIES:
Under general supervision, performs expert-level and complex work involving the diagnoses, troubleshooting, adjustment and repair of electric and hydraulic passenger or freight elevators, escalators, and associated electromechanical equipment in MTA Transit stations, shops, buildings and yards; utilizes state-of-the-art technology, analytical and diagnostic tools, and facilities management and maintenance related software; prepares reports; drives a motor vehicle to transport material, equipment and personnel to and from various worksites; and performs related work.

SCOPE OF THE EXAMINATIONS:
The qualifying multiple-choice test may include questions on advanced knowledge of electrical theory and electronic controls; advanced knowledge of electrical, mechanical, and hydraulic elevator and escalator devices and components; advanced diagnostic, trouble-shooting and repair procedures; safe, proper and efficient work practices; reading and interpreting complex schematics, blueprints and drawings; keeping records; and other related areas.

The competitive practical skills test may include tasks related to advanced trouble-shooting and repair of electrical, electronic, mechanical, and electromechanical components and systems of elevators and escalators, including the selection and use of appropriate tools, meters and materials; reading and interpreting complex technical drawings; shop math; safe work practices and procedures; and other related areas.

HOW TO TAKE A TEST

I. YOU MUST PASS AN EXAMINATION

A. *WHAT EVERY CANDIDATE SHOULD KNOW*

Examination applicants often ask us for help in preparing for the written test. What can I study in advance? What kinds of questions will be asked? How will the test be given? How will the papers be graded?

As an applicant for a civil service examination, you may be wondering about some of these things. Our purpose here is to suggest effective methods of advance study and to describe civil service examinations.

Your chances for success on this examination can be increased if you know how to prepare. Those "pre-examination jitters" can be reduced if you know what to expect. You can even experience an adventure in good citizenship if you know why civil service exams are given.

B. *WHY ARE CIVIL SERVICE EXAMINATIONS GIVEN?*

Civil service examinations are important to you in two ways. As a citizen, you want public jobs filled by employees who know how to do their work. As a job seeker, you want a fair chance to compete for that job on an equal footing with other candidates. The best-known means of accomplishing this two-fold goal is the competitive examination.

Exams are widely publicized throughout the nation. They may be administered for jobs in federal, state, city, municipal, town or village governments or agencies.

Any citizen may apply, with some limitations, such as the age or residence of applicants. Your experience and education may be reviewed to see whether you meet the requirements for the particular examination. When these requirements exist, they are reasonable and applied consistently to all applicants. Thus, a competitive examination may cause you some uneasiness now, but it is your privilege and safeguard.

C. *HOW ARE CIVIL SERVICE EXAMS DEVELOPED?*

Examinations are carefully written by trained technicians who are specialists in the field known as "psychological measurement," in consultation with recognized authorities in the field of work that the test will cover. These experts recommend the subject matter areas or skills to be tested; only those knowledges or skills important to your success on the job are included. The most reliable books and source materials available are used as references. Together, the experts and technicians judge the difficulty level of the questions.

Test technicians know how to phrase questions so that the problem is clearly stated. Their ethics do not permit "trick" or "catch" questions. Questions may have been tried out on sample groups, or subjected to statistical analysis, to determine their usefulness.

Written tests are often used in combination with performance tests, ratings of training and experience, and oral interviews. All of these measures combine to form the best-known means of finding the right person for the right job.

II. HOW TO PASS THE WRITTEN TEST

A. NATURE OF THE EXAMINATION

To prepare intelligently for civil service examinations, you should know how they differ from school examinations you have taken. In school you were assigned certain definite pages to read or subjects to cover. The examination questions were quite detailed and usually emphasized memory. Civil service exams, on the other hand, try to discover your present ability to perform the duties of a position, plus your potentiality to learn these duties. In other words, a civil service exam attempts to predict how successful you will be. Questions cover such a broad area that they cannot be as minute and detailed as school exam questions.

In the public service similar kinds of work, or positions, are grouped together in one "class." This process is known as *position-classification*. All the positions in a class are paid according to the salary range for that class. One class title covers all of these positions, and they are all tested by the same examination.

B. FOUR BASIC STEPS

1) Study the announcement

How, then, can you know what subjects to study? Our best answer is: "Learn as much as possible about the class of positions for which you've applied." The exam will test the knowledge, skills and abilities needed to do the work.

Your most valuable source of information about the position you want is the official exam announcement. This announcement lists the training and experience qualifications. Check these standards and apply only if you come reasonably close to meeting them.

The brief description of the position in the examination announcement offers some clues to the subjects which will be tested. Think about the job itself. Review the duties in your mind. Can you perform them, or are there some in which you are rusty? Fill in the blank spots in your preparation.

Many jurisdictions preview the written test in the exam announcement by including a section called "Knowledge and Abilities Required," "Scope of the Examination," or some similar heading. Here you will find out specifically what fields will be tested.

2) Review your own background

Once you learn in general what the position is all about, and what you need to know to do the work, ask yourself which subjects you already know fairly well and which need improvement. You may wonder whether to concentrate on improving your strong areas or on building some background in your fields of weakness. When the announcement has specified "some knowledge" or "considerable knowledge," or has used adjectives like "beginning principles of…" or "advanced … methods," you can get a clue as to the number and difficulty of questions to be asked in any given field. More questions, and hence broader coverage, would be included for those subjects which are more important in the work. Now weigh your strengths and weaknesses against the job requirements and prepare accordingly.

3) Determine the level of the position

Another way to tell how intensively you should prepare is to understand the level of the job for which you are applying. Is it the entering level? In other words, is this the position in which beginners in a field of work are hired? Or is it an intermediate or advanced level? Sometimes this is indicated by such words as "Junior" or "Senior" in the class title. Other jurisdictions use Roman numerals to designate the level – Clerk I, Clerk II, for example. The word "Supervisor" sometimes appears in the title. If the level is not indicated by the title, check the description of duties. Will you be working under very close supervision, or will you have responsibility for independent decisions in this work?

4) Choose appropriate study materials

Now that you know the subjects to be examined and the relative amount of each subject to be covered, you can choose suitable study materials. For beginning level jobs, or even advanced ones, if you have a pronounced weakness in some aspect of your training, read a modern, standard textbook in that field. Be sure it is up to date and has general coverage. Such books are normally available at your library, and the librarian will be glad to help you locate one. For entry-level positions, questions of appropriate difficulty are chosen – neither highly advanced questions, nor those too simple. Such questions require careful thought but not advanced training.

If the position for which you are applying is technical or advanced, you will read more advanced, specialized material. If you are already familiar with the basic principles of your field, elementary textbooks would waste your time. Concentrate on advanced textbooks and technical periodicals. Think through the concepts and review difficult problems in your field.

These are all general sources. You can get more ideas on your own initiative, following these leads. For example, training manuals and publications of the government agency which employs workers in your field can be useful, particularly for technical and professional positions. A letter or visit to the government department involved may result in more specific study suggestions, and certainly will provide you with a more definite idea of the exact nature of the position you are seeking.

III. KINDS OF TESTS

Tests are used for purposes other than measuring knowledge and ability to perform specified duties. For some positions, it is equally important to test ability to make adjustments to new situations or to profit from training. In others, basic mental abilities not dependent on information are essential. Questions which test these things may not appear as pertinent to the duties of the position as those which test for knowledge and information. Yet they are often highly important parts of a fair examination. For very general questions, it is almost impossible to help you direct your study efforts. What we can do is to point out some of the more common of these general abilities needed in public service positions and describe some typical questions.

1) General information

Broad, general information has been found useful for predicting job success in some kinds of work. This is tested in a variety of ways, from vocabulary lists to questions about current events. Basic background in some field of work, such as sociology or economics, may be sampled in a group of questions. Often these are principles which have become familiar to most persons through exposure rather than through formal training. It is difficult to advise you how to study for these questions; being alert to the world around you is our best suggestion.

2) Verbal ability

An example of an ability needed in many positions is verbal or language ability. Verbal ability is, in brief, the ability to use and understand words. Vocabulary and grammar tests are typical measures of this ability. Reading comprehension or paragraph interpretation questions are common in many kinds of civil service tests. You are given a paragraph of written material and asked to find its central meaning.

3) Numerical ability

Number skills can be tested by the familiar arithmetic problem, by checking paired lists of numbers to see which are alike and which are different, or by interpreting charts and graphs. In the latter test, a graph may be printed in the test booklet which you are asked to use as the basis for answering questions.

4) Observation

A popular test for law-enforcement positions is the observation test. A picture is shown to you for several minutes, then taken away. Questions about the picture test your ability to observe both details and larger elements.

5) Following directions

In many positions in the public service, the employee must be able to carry out written instructions dependably and accurately. You may be given a chart with several columns, each column listing a variety of information. The questions require you to carry out directions involving the information given in the chart.

6) Skills and aptitudes

Performance tests effectively measure some manual skills and aptitudes. When the skill is one in which you are trained, such as typing or shorthand, you can practice. These tests are often very much like those given in business school or high school courses. For many of the other skills and aptitudes, however, no short-time preparation can be made. Skills and abilities natural to you or that you have developed throughout your lifetime are being tested.

Many of the general questions just described provide all the data needed to answer the questions and ask you to use your reasoning ability to find the answers. Your best preparation for these tests, as well as for tests of facts and ideas, is to be at your physical and mental best. You, no doubt, have your own methods of getting into an exam-taking mood and keeping "in shape." The next section lists some ideas on this subject.

IV. KINDS OF QUESTIONS

Only rarely is the "essay" question, which you answer in narrative form, used in civil service tests. Civil service tests are usually of the short-answer type. Full instructions for answering these questions will be given to you at the examination. But in case this is your first experience with short-answer questions and separate answer sheets, here is what you need to know:

1) Multiple-choice Questions

Most popular of the short-answer questions is the "multiple choice" or "best answer" question. It can be used, for example, to test for factual knowledge, ability to solve problems or judgment in meeting situations found at work.

A multiple-choice question is normally one of three types—
- It can begin with an incomplete statement followed by several possible endings. You are to find the one ending which *best* completes the statement, although some of the others may not be entirely wrong.
- It can also be a complete statement in the form of a question which is answered by choosing one of the statements listed.

- It can be in the form of a problem – again you select the best answer.

Here is an example of a multiple-choice question with a discussion which should give you some clues as to the method for choosing the right answer:

When an employee has a complaint about his assignment, the action which will *best* help him overcome his difficulty is to
  A. discuss his difficulty with his coworkers
  B. take the problem to the head of the organization
  C. take the problem to the person who gave him the assignment
  D. say nothing to anyone about his complaint

In answering this question, you should study each of the choices to find which is best. Consider choice "A" – Certainly an employee may discuss his complaint with fellow employees, but no change or improvement can result, and the complaint remains unresolved. Choice "B" is a poor choice since the head of the organization probably does not know what assignment you have been given, and taking your problem to him is known as "going over the head" of the supervisor. The supervisor, or person who made the assignment, is the person who can clarify it or correct any injustice. Choice "C" is, therefore, correct. To say nothing, as in choice "D," is unwise. Supervisors have and interest in knowing the problems employees are facing, and the employee is seeking a solution to his problem.

2) True/False Questions

The "true/false" or "right/wrong" form of question is sometimes used. Here a complete statement is given. Your job is to decide whether the statement is right or wrong.

SAMPLE: A roaming cell-phone call to a nearby city costs less than a non-roaming call to a distant city.

This statement is wrong, or false, since roaming calls are more expensive.

This is not a complete list of all possible question forms, although most of the others are variations of these common types. You will always get complete directions for answering questions. Be sure you understand *how* to mark your answers – ask questions until you do.

V. RECORDING YOUR ANSWERS

Computer terminals are used more and more today for many different kinds of exams.

For an examination with very few applicants, you may be told to record your answers in the test booklet itself. Separate answer sheets are much more common. If this separate answer sheet is to be scored by machine – and this is often the case – it is highly important that you mark your answers correctly in order to get credit.

An electronic scoring machine is often used in civil service offices because of the speed with which papers can be scored. Machine-scored answer sheets must be marked with a pencil, which will be given to you. This pencil has a high graphite content which responds to the electronic scoring machine. As a matter of fact, stray dots may register as answers, so do not let your pencil rest on the answer sheet while you are pondering the correct answer. Also, if your pencil lead breaks or is otherwise defective, ask for another.

Since the answer sheet will be dropped in a slot in the scoring machine, be careful not to bend the corners or get the paper crumpled.

The answer sheet normally has five vertical columns of numbers, with 30 numbers to a column. These numbers correspond to the question numbers in your test booklet. After each number, going across the page are four or five pairs of dotted lines. These short dotted lines have small letters or numbers above them. The first two pairs may also have a "T" or "F" above the letters. This indicates that the first two pairs only are to be used if the questions are of the true-false type. If the questions are multiple choice, disregard the "T" and "F" and pay attention only to the small letters or numbers.

Answer your questions in the manner of the sample that follows:

32. The largest city in the United States is
    A. Washington, D.C.
    B. New York City
    C. Chicago
    D. Detroit
    E. San Francisco

1) Choose the answer you think is best. (New York City is the largest, so "B" is correct.)
2) Find the row of dotted lines numbered the same as the question you are answering. (Find row number 32)
3) Find the pair of dotted lines corresponding to the answer. (Find the pair of lines under the mark "B.")
4) Make a solid black mark between the dotted lines.

VI. BEFORE THE TEST

Common sense will help you find procedures to follow to get ready for an examination. Too many of us, however, overlook these sensible measures. Indeed, nervousness and fatigue have been found to be the most serious reasons why applicants fail to do their best on civil service tests. Here is a list of reminders:

- Begin your preparation early – Don't wait until the last minute to go scurrying around for books and materials or to find out what the position is all about.
- Prepare continuously – An hour a night for a week is better than an all-night cram session. This has been definitely established. What is more, a night a week for a month will return better dividends than crowding your study into a shorter period of time.
- Locate the place of the exam – You have been sent a notice telling you when and where to report for the examination. If the location is in a different town or otherwise unfamiliar to you, it would be well to inquire the best route and learn something about the building.
- Relax the night before the test – Allow your mind to rest. Do not study at all that night. Plan some mild recreation or diversion; then go to bed early and get a good night's sleep.
- Get up early enough to make a leisurely trip to the place for the test – This way unforeseen events, traffic snarls, unfamiliar buildings, etc. will not upset you.
- Dress comfortably – A written test is not a fashion show. You will be known by number and not by name, so wear something comfortable.

- Leave excess paraphernalia at home – Shopping bags and odd bundles will get in your way. You need bring only the items mentioned in the official notice you received; usually everything you need is provided. Do not bring reference books to the exam. They will only confuse those last minutes and be taken away from you when in the test room.
- Arrive somewhat ahead of time – If because of transportation schedules you must get there very early, bring a newspaper or magazine to take your mind off yourself while waiting.
- Locate the examination room – When you have found the proper room, you will be directed to the seat or part of the room where you will sit. Sometimes you are given a sheet of instructions to read while you are waiting. Do not fill out any forms until you are told to do so; just read them and be prepared.
- Relax and prepare to listen to the instructions
- If you have any physical problem that may keep you from doing your best, be sure to tell the test administrator. If you are sick or in poor health, you really cannot do your best on the exam. You can come back and take the test some other time.

VII. AT THE TEST

The day of the test is here and you have the test booklet in your hand. The temptation to get going is very strong. Caution! There is more to success than knowing the right answers. You must know how to identify your papers and understand variations in the type of short-answer question used in this particular examination. Follow these suggestions for maximum results from your efforts:

1) Cooperate with the monitor

The test administrator has a duty to create a situation in which you can be as much at ease as possible. He will give instructions, tell you when to begin, check to see that you are marking your answer sheet correctly, and so on. He is not there to guard you, although he will see that your competitors do not take unfair advantage. He wants to help you do your best.

2) Listen to all instructions

Don't jump the gun! Wait until you understand all directions. In most civil service tests you get more time than you need to answer the questions. So don't be in a hurry. Read each word of instructions until you clearly understand the meaning. Study the examples, listen to all announcements and follow directions. Ask questions if you do not understand what to do.

3) Identify your papers

Civil service exams are usually identified by number only. You will be assigned a number; you must not put your name on your test papers. Be sure to copy your number correctly. Since more than one exam may be given, copy your exact examination title.

4) Plan your time

Unless you are told that a test is a "speed" or "rate of work" test, speed itself is usually not important. Time enough to answer all the questions will be provided, but this does not mean that you have all day. An overall time limit has been set. Divide the total time (in minutes) by the number of questions to determine the approximate time you have for each question.

5) Do not linger over difficult questions

If you come across a difficult question, mark it with a paper clip (useful to have along) and come back to it when you have been through the booklet. One caution if you do this – be sure to skip a number on your answer sheet as well. Check often to be sure that you have not lost your place and that you are marking in the row numbered the same as the question you are answering.

6) Read the questions

Be sure you know what the question asks! Many capable people are unsuccessful because they failed to *read* the questions correctly.

7) Answer all questions

Unless you have been instructed that a penalty will be deducted for incorrect answers, it is better to guess than to omit a question.

8) Speed tests

It is often better NOT to guess on speed tests. It has been found that on timed tests people are tempted to spend the last few seconds before time is called in marking answers at random – without even reading them – in the hope of picking up a few extra points. To discourage this practice, the instructions may warn you that your score will be "corrected" for guessing. That is, a penalty will be applied. The incorrect answers will be deducted from the correct ones, or some other penalty formula will be used.

9) Review your answers

If you finish before time is called, go back to the questions you guessed or omitted to give them further thought. Review other answers if you have time.

10) Return your test materials

If you are ready to leave before others have finished or time is called, take ALL your materials to the monitor and leave quietly. Never take any test material with you. The monitor can discover whose papers are not complete, and taking a test booklet may be grounds for disqualification.

VIII. EXAMINATION TECHNIQUES

1) Read the general instructions carefully. These are usually printed on the first page of the exam booklet. As a rule, these instructions refer to the timing of the examination; the fact that you should not start work until the signal and must stop work at a signal, etc. If there are any *special* instructions, such as a choice of questions to be answered, make sure that you note this instruction carefully.

2) When you are ready to start work on the examination, that is as soon as the signal has been given, read the instructions to each question booklet, underline any key words or phrases, such as *least, best, outline, describe* and the like. In this way you will tend to answer as requested rather than discover on reviewing your paper that you *listed without describing*, that you selected the *worst* choice rather than the *best* choice, etc.

3) If the examination is of the objective or multiple-choice type – that is, each question will also give a series of possible answers: A, B, C or D, and you are called upon to select the best answer and write the letter next to that answer on your answer paper – it is advisable to start answering each question in turn. There may be anywhere from 50 to 100 such questions in the three or four hours allotted and you can see how much time would be taken if you read through all the questions before beginning to answer any. Furthermore, if you come across a question or group of questions which you know would be difficult to answer, it would undoubtedly affect your handling of all the other questions.

4) If the examination is of the essay type and contains but a few questions, it is a moot point as to whether you should read all the questions before starting to answer any one. Of course, if you are given a choice – say five out of seven and the like – then it is essential to read all the questions so you can eliminate the two that are most difficult. If, however, you are asked to answer all the questions, there may be danger in trying to answer the easiest one first because you may find that you will spend too much time on it. The best technique is to answer the first question, then proceed to the second, etc.

5) Time your answers. Before the exam begins, write down the time it started, then add the time allowed for the examination and write down the time it must be completed, then divide the time available somewhat as follows:
    - If 3-1/2 hours are allowed, that would be 210 minutes. If you have 80 objective-type questions, that would be an average of 2-1/2 minutes per question. Allow yourself no more than 2 minutes per question, or a total of 160 minutes, which will permit about 50 minutes to review.
    - If for the time allotment of 210 minutes there are 7 essay questions to answer, that would average about 30 minutes a question. Give yourself only 25 minutes per question so that you have about 35 minutes to review.

6) The most important instruction is to *read each question* and make sure you know what is wanted. The second most important instruction is to *time yourself properly* so that you answer every question. The third most important instruction is to *answer every question*. Guess if you have to but include something for each question. Remember that you will receive no credit for a blank and will probably receive some credit if you write something in answer to an essay question. If you guess a letter – say "B" for a multiple-choice question – you may have guessed right. If you leave a blank as an answer to a multiple-choice question, the examiners may respect your feelings but it will not add a point to your score. Some exams may penalize you for wrong answers, so in such cases *only*, you may not want to guess unless you have some basis for your answer.

7) Suggestions
    a. Objective-type questions
        1. Examine the question booklet for proper sequence of pages and questions
        2. Read all instructions carefully
        3. Skip any question which seems too difficult; return to it after all other questions have been answered
        4. Apportion your time properly; do not spend too much time on any single question or group of questions

5. Note and underline key words – *all, most, fewest, least, best, worst, same, opposite*, etc.
6. Pay particular attention to negatives
7. Note unusual option, e.g., unduly long, short, complex, different or similar in content to the body of the question
8. Observe the use of "hedging" words – *probably, may, most likely*, etc.
9. Make sure that your answer is put next to the same number as the question
10. Do not second-guess unless you have good reason to believe the second answer is definitely more correct
11. Cross out original answer if you decide another answer is more accurate; do not erase until you are ready to hand your paper in
12. Answer all questions; guess unless instructed otherwise
13. Leave time for review

b. Essay questions
1. Read each question carefully
2. Determine exactly what is wanted. Underline key words or phrases.
3. Decide on outline or paragraph answer
4. Include many different points and elements unless asked to develop any one or two points or elements
5. Show impartiality by giving pros and cons unless directed to select one side only
6. Make and write down any assumptions you find necessary to answer the questions
7. Watch your English, grammar, punctuation and choice of words
8. Time your answers; don't crowd material

8) Answering the essay question

Most essay questions can be answered by framing the specific response around several key words or ideas. Here are a few such key words or ideas:

M's: manpower, materials, methods, money, management
P's: purpose, program, policy, plan, procedure, practice, problems, pitfalls, personnel, public relations

a. Six basic steps in handling problems:
1. Preliminary plan and background development
2. Collect information, data and facts
3. Analyze and interpret information, data and facts
4. Analyze and develop solutions as well as make recommendations
5. Prepare report and sell recommendations
6. Install recommendations and follow up effectiveness

b. Pitfalls to avoid
1. *Taking things for granted* – A statement of the situation does not necessarily imply that each of the elements is necessarily true; for example, a complaint may be invalid and biased so that all that can be taken for granted is that a complaint has been registered

2. *Considering only one side of a situation* – Wherever possible, indicate several alternatives and then point out the reasons you selected the best one
3. *Failing to indicate follow up* – Whenever your answer indicates action on your part, make certain that you will take proper follow-up action to see how successful your recommendations, procedures or actions turn out to be
4. *Taking too long in answering any single question* – Remember to time your answers properly

IX. AFTER THE TEST

Scoring procedures differ in detail among civil service jurisdictions although the general principles are the same. Whether the papers are hand-scored or graded by machine we have described, they are nearly always graded by number. That is, the person who marks the paper knows only the number – never the name – of the applicant. Not until all the papers have been graded will they be matched with names. If other tests, such as training and experience or oral interview ratings have been given, scores will be combined. Different parts of the examination usually have different weights. For example, the written test might count 60 percent of the final grade, and a rating of training and experience 40 percent. In many jurisdictions, veterans will have a certain number of points added to their grades.

After the final grade has been determined, the names are placed in grade order and an eligible list is established. There are various methods for resolving ties between those who get the same final grade – probably the most common is to place first the name of the person whose application was received first. Job offers are made from the eligible list in the order the names appear on it. You will be notified of your grade and your rank as soon as all these computations have been made. This will be done as rapidly as possible.

People who are found to meet the requirements in the announcement are called "eligibles." Their names are put on a list of eligible candidates. An eligible's chances of getting a job depend on how high he stands on this list and how fast agencies are filling jobs from the list.

When a job is to be filled from a list of eligibles, the agency asks for the names of people on the list of eligibles for that job. When the civil service commission receives this request, it sends to the agency the names of the three people highest on this list. Or, if the job to be filled has specialized requirements, the office sends the agency the names of the top three persons who meet these requirements from the general list.

The appointing officer makes a choice from among the three people whose names were sent to him. If the selected person accepts the appointment, the names of the others are put back on the list to be considered for future openings.

That is the rule in hiring from all kinds of eligible lists, whether they are for typist, carpenter, chemist, or something else. For every vacancy, the appointing officer has his choice of any one of the top three eligibles on the list. This explains why the person whose name is on top of the list sometimes does not get an appointment when some of the persons lower on the list do. If the appointing officer chooses the second or third eligible, the No. 1 eligible does not get a job at once, but stays on the list until he is appointed or the list is terminated.

X. HOW TO PASS THE INTERVIEW TEST

The examination for which you applied requires an oral interview test. You have already taken the written test and you are now being called for the interview test – the final part of the formal examination.

You may think that it is not possible to prepare for an interview test and that there are no procedures to follow during an interview. Our purpose is to point out some things you can do in advance that will help you and some good rules to follow and pitfalls to avoid while you are being interviewed.

What is an interview supposed to test?

The written examination is designed to test the technical knowledge and competence of the candidate; the oral is designed to evaluate intangible qualities, not readily measured otherwise, and to establish a list showing the relative fitness of each candidate – as measured against his competitors – for the position sought. Scoring is not on the basis of "right" and "wrong," but on a sliding scale of values ranging from "not passable" to "outstanding." As a matter of fact, it is possible to achieve a relatively low score without a single "incorrect" answer because of evident weakness in the qualities being measured.

Occasionally, an examination may consist entirely of an oral test – either an individual or a group oral. In such cases, information is sought concerning the technical knowledges and abilities of the candidate, since there has been no written examination for this purpose. More commonly, however, an oral test is used to supplement a written examination.

Who conducts interviews?

The composition of oral boards varies among different jurisdictions. In nearly all, a representative of the personnel department serves as chairman. One of the members of the board may be a representative of the department in which the candidate would work. In some cases, "outside experts" are used, and, frequently, a businessman or some other representative of the general public is asked to serve. Labor and management or other special groups may be represented. The aim is to secure the services of experts in the appropriate field.

However the board is composed, it is a good idea (and not at all improper or unethical) to ascertain in advance of the interview who the members are and what groups they represent. When you are introduced to them, you will have some idea of their backgrounds and interests, and at least you will not stutter and stammer over their names.

What should be done before the interview?

While knowledge about the board members is useful and takes some of the surprise element out of the interview, there is other preparation which is more substantive. It *is* possible to prepare for an oral interview – in several ways:

1) Keep a copy of your application and review it carefully before the interview

This may be the only document before the oral board, and the starting point of the interview. Know what education and experience you have listed there, and the sequence and dates of all of it. Sometimes the board will ask you to review the highlights of your experience for them; you should not have to hem and haw doing it.

2) Study the class specification and the examination announcement

Usually, the oral board has one or both of these to guide them. The qualities, characteristics or knowledges required by the position sought are stated in these documents. They offer valuable clues as to the nature of the oral interview. For example, if the job involves supervisory responsibilities, the announcement will usually indicate that knowledge of modern supervisory methods and the qualifications of the candidate as a supervisor will be tested. If so, you can expect such questions, frequently in the form of a hypothetical situation which you are expected to solve. NEVER go into an oral without knowledge of the duties and responsibilities of the job you seek.

3) Think through each qualification required

Try to visualize the kind of questions you would ask if you were a board member. How well could you answer them? Try especially to appraise your own knowledge and background in each area, *measured against the job sought*, and identify any areas in which you are weak. Be critical and realistic – do not flatter yourself.

4) Do some general reading in areas in which you feel you may be weak

For example, if the job involves supervision and your past experience has NOT, some general reading in supervisory methods and practices, particularly in the field of human relations, might be useful. Do NOT study agency procedures or detailed manuals. The oral board will be testing your understanding and capacity, not your memory.

5) Get a good night's sleep and watch your general health and mental attitude

You will want a clear head at the interview. Take care of a cold or any other minor ailment, and of course, no hangovers.

What should be done on the day of the interview?

Now comes the day of the interview itself. Give yourself plenty of time to get there. Plan to arrive somewhat ahead of the scheduled time, particularly if your appointment is in the fore part of the day. If a previous candidate fails to appear, the board might be ready for you a bit early. By early afternoon an oral board is almost invariably behind schedule if there are many candidates, and you may have to wait. Take along a book or magazine to read, or your application to review, but leave any extraneous material in the waiting room when you go in for your interview. In any event, relax and compose yourself.

The matter of dress is important. The board is forming impressions about you – from your experience, your manners, your attitude, and your appearance. Give your personal appearance careful attention. Dress your best, but not your flashiest. Choose conservative, appropriate clothing, and be sure it is immaculate. This is a business interview, and your appearance should indicate that you regard it as such. Besides, being well groomed and properly dressed will help boost your confidence.

Sooner or later, someone will call your name and escort you into the interview room. *This is it.* From here on you are on your own. It is too late for any more preparation. But remember, you asked for this opportunity to prove your fitness, and you are here because your request was granted.

What happens when you go in?

The usual sequence of events will be as follows: The clerk (who is often the board stenographer) will introduce you to the chairman of the oral board, who will introduce you to the other members of the board. Acknowledge the introductions before you sit down. Do not be surprised if you find a microphone facing you or a stenotypist sitting by. Oral interviews are usually recorded in the event of an appeal or other review.

Usually the chairman of the board will open the interview by reviewing the highlights of your education and work experience from your application – primarily for the benefit of the other members of the board, as well as to get the material into the record. Do not interrupt or comment unless there is an error or significant misinterpretation; if that is the case, do not hesitate. But do not quibble about insignificant matters. Also, he will usually ask you some question about your education, experience or your present job – partly to get you to start talking and to establish the interviewing "rapport." He may start the actual questioning, or turn it over to one of the other members. Frequently, each member undertakes the questioning on a particular area, one in which he is perhaps most competent, so you can expect each member to participate in the examination. Because time is limited, you may also expect some rather abrupt switches in the direction the questioning takes, so do not be upset by it. Normally, a board member will not pursue a single line of questioning unless he discovers a particular strength or weakness.

After each member has participated, the chairman will usually ask whether any member has any further questions, then will ask you if you have anything you wish to add. Unless you are expecting this question, it may floor you. Worse, it may start you off on an extended, extemporaneous speech. The board is not usually seeking more information. The question is principally to offer you a last opportunity to present further qualifications or to indicate that you have nothing to add. So, if you feel that a significant qualification or characteristic has been overlooked, it is proper to point it out in a sentence or so. Do not compliment the board on the thoroughness of their examination – they have been sketchy, and you know it. If you wish, merely say, "No thank you, I have nothing further to add." This is a point where you can "talk yourself out" of a good impression or fail to present an important bit of information. Remember, *you close the interview yourself*.

The chairman will then say, "That is all, Mr. _____, thank you." Do not be startled; the interview is over, and quicker than you think. Thank him, gather your belongings and take your leave. Save your sigh of relief for the other side of the door.

How to put your best foot forward
Throughout this entire process, you may feel that the board individually and collectively is trying to pierce your defenses, seek out your hidden weaknesses and embarrass and confuse you. Actually, this is not true. They are obliged to make an appraisal of your qualifications for the job you are seeking, and they want to see you in your best light. Remember, they must interview all candidates and a non-cooperative candidate may become a failure in spite of their best efforts to bring out his qualifications. Here are 15 suggestions that will help you:

1) **Be natural – Keep your attitude confident, not cocky**
If you are not confident that you can do the job, do not expect the board to be. Do not apologize for your weaknesses, try to bring out your strong points. The board is interested in a positive, not negative, presentation. Cockiness will antagonize any board member and make him wonder if you are covering up a weakness by a false show of strength.

2) **Get comfortable, but don't lounge or sprawl**
Sit erectly but not stiffly. A careless posture may lead the board to conclude that you are careless in other things, or at least that you are not impressed by the importance of the occasion. Either conclusion is natural, even if incorrect. Do not fuss with your clothing, a pencil or an ashtray. Your hands may occasionally be useful to emphasize a point; do not let them become a point of distraction.

3) **Do not wisecrack or make small talk**
This is a serious situation, and your attitude should show that you consider it as such. Further, the time of the board is limited – they do not want to waste it, and neither should you.

4) Do not exaggerate your experience or abilities
In the first place, from information in the application or other interviews and sources, the board may know more about you than you think. Secondly, you probably will not get away with it. An experienced board is rather adept at spotting such a situation, so do not take the chance.

5) If you know a board member, do not make a point of it, yet do not hide it
Certainly you are not fooling him, and probably not the other members of the board. Do not try to take advantage of your acquaintanceship – it will probably do you little good.

6) Do not dominate the interview
Let the board do that. They will give you the clues – do not assume that you have to do all the talking. Realize that the board has a number of questions to ask you, and do not try to take up all the interview time by showing off your extensive knowledge of the answer to the first one.

7) Be attentive
You only have 20 minutes or so, and you should keep your attention at its sharpest throughout. When a member is addressing a problem or question to you, give him your undivided attention. Address your reply principally to him, but do not exclude the other board members.

8) Do not interrupt
A board member may be stating a problem for you to analyze. He will ask you a question when the time comes. Let him state the problem, and wait for the question.

9) Make sure you understand the question
Do not try to answer until you are sure what the question is. If it is not clear, restate it in your own words or ask the board member to clarify it for you. However, do not haggle about minor elements.

10) Reply promptly but not hastily
A common entry on oral board rating sheets is "candidate responded readily," or "candidate hesitated in replies." Respond as promptly and quickly as you can, but do not jump to a hasty, ill-considered answer.

11) Do not be peremptory in your answers
A brief answer is proper – but do not fire your answer back. That is a losing game from your point of view. The board member can probably ask questions much faster than you can answer them.

12) Do not try to create the answer you think the board member wants
He is interested in what kind of mind you have and how it works – not in playing games. Furthermore, he can usually spot this practice and will actually grade you down on it.

13) Do not switch sides in your reply merely to agree with a board member
Frequently, a member will take a contrary position merely to draw you out and to see if you are willing and able to defend your point of view. Do not start a debate, yet do not surrender a good position. If a position is worth taking, it is worth defending.

14) Do not be afraid to admit an error in judgment if you are shown to be wrong

The board knows that you are forced to reply without any opportunity for careful consideration. Your answer may be demonstrably wrong. If so, admit it and get on with the interview.

15) Do not dwell at length on your present job

The opening question may relate to your present assignment. Answer the question but do not go into an extended discussion. You are being examined for a *new* job, not your present one. As a matter of fact, try to phrase ALL your answers in terms of the job for which you are being examined.

Basis of Rating

Probably you will forget most of these "do's" and "don'ts" when you walk into the oral interview room. Even remembering them all will not ensure you a passing grade. Perhaps you did not have the qualifications in the first place. But remembering them will help you to put your best foot forward, without treading on the toes of the board members.

Rumor and popular opinion to the contrary notwithstanding, an oral board wants you to make the best appearance possible. They know you are under pressure – but they also want to see how you respond to it as a guide to what your reaction would be under the pressures of the job you seek. They will be influenced by the degree of poise you display, the personal traits you show and the manner in which you respond.

ABOUT THIS BOOK

This book contains tests divided into Examination Sections. Go through each test, answering every question in the margin. We have also attached a sample answer sheet at the back of the book that can be removed and used. At the end of each test look at the answer key and check your answers. On the ones you got wrong, look at the right answer choice and learn. Do not fill in the answers first. Do not memorize the questions and answers, but understand the answer and principles involved. On your test, the questions will likely be different from the samples. Questions are changed and new ones added. If you understand these past questions you should have success with any changes that arise. Tests may consist of several types of questions. We have additional books on each subject should more study be advisable or necessary for you. Finally, the more you study, the better prepared you will be. This book is intended to be the last thing you study before you walk into the examination room. Prior study of relevant texts is also recommended. NLC publishes some of these in our Fundamental Series. Knowledge and good sense are important factors in passing your exam. Good luck also helps. So now study this Passbook, absorb the material contained within and take that knowledge into the examination. Then do your best to pass that exam.

EXAMINATION SECTION

EXAMINATION SECTION
TEST 1

DIRECTIONS: Each question or incomplete statement is followed by several suggested answers or completions. Select the one that BEST answers the question or completes the statement. *PRINT THE LETTER OF THE CORRECT ANSWER IN THE SPACE AT THE RIGHT.*

1. The one of the following which is a unit of inductance is the   1._____
   A. millihenry   B. microfarad   C. kilohm   D. weber

2. Of the following, the BEST conductor of electricity is   2._____
   A. aluminum   B. copper   C. silver   D. iron

3. A voltage of 1000 microvolts is the SAME as   3._____
   A. 1,000 volts   B. 0.100 volts
   C. 0.010 volts   D. 0.001 volts

4. The function of a rectifier is SIMILAR to that of a(n)   4._____
   A. inverter   B. relay   C. commutator   D. transformer

5. A 9-ohm resistor rated at 225 watts is used in a 120-volt circuit. In order not to exceed the rating of the resistor, the MAXIMUM current, in amperes, which can flow through the circuit is   5._____
   A. 2   B. 3   C. 4   D. 5

6. The number of circular mils in a conductor 0.036 inch in diameter is   6._____
   A. 6   B. 36   C. 72   D. 1296

7. The color of the label on most commercially available 250-volt cartridge fuses of 15-amperes or less capacity is   7._____
   A. green   B. blue   C. red   D. yellow

8. Assume that a two-microfarad capacitor is connected in parallel with a three-microfarad capacitor. The resulting capacity, in microfarads, is   8._____
   A. 2/3   B. 6/5   C. 3/2   D. 5

9. The speed of the rotating magnetic field in a 12-pole 60-cycle stator is   9._____
   A. 1800 rpm   B. 1200 rpm   C. 720 rpm   D. D 600 rpm

10. The transformer connection *generally* used to convert from three-phase to two-phase by means of two transformers is the   10._____
    A. Scott or T   B. V or Open delta
    C. Wye-Delta   D. Delta-Wye

11. The conductance, in mhos, of a circuit whose resistance is one ohm is

    A. 1/10 B. 1 C. 10 D. 100

12. Assume that a 220-volt, 25 cycle, A.C., e.m.f. is impressed across a circuit consisting of a 25-ohm resistor in series with a 30-microfarad capacitor. The current in this circuit, in amperes, is, *most nearly,*

    A. 0.5 B. 0.8 C. 1.0 D. 1.5

13. An ammeter has a full scale deflection with a current of 0.010 amperes and an internal resistance of 20 ohms.
    In order for the ammeter to have a full scale deflection with a current of 10 amperes and not damage its movement, a shunt should be used having a value of

    A. 10 ohms B. 0.2 ohms C. 0.02 ohms D. 0.01 ohms

14. American Wire Gage (A.W.G.) wire size numbers are set so that the resistance of wire per 1,000 ft. doubles with every increase of

    A. one gage number
    B. two gage numbers
    C. three gage numbers
    D. four gage numbers

15. In an ideal transformer for transforming or "stepping down" the voltage from 1200 volts to 120 volts, the turns ratio is

    A. 10:1 B. 12:1 C. 1:12 D. 1:10

16. When a lead-acid battery is fully charged, the negative plate consists of lead

    A. peroxide B. sponge C. sulfate D. dioxide

17. Improving the commutation of a D.C. generator is MOST often done by using

    A. a rheostat in series with the equalizer
    B. an equalizer alone
    C. a compensator
    D. interpoles

18. In a wave-wound armature, the MINIMUM number of commutator brushes necessary is

    A. two times the number of poles
    B. two, regardless of the number of poles
    C. one-half times the number of poles
    D. four, regardless of the number of poles

19. A three-phase induction motor runs hot with all stator coils at the same temperature. The trouble which would cause this condition is that

    A. the motor is running single phase
    B. the motor is overloaded
    C. a part of the motor windings is inoperative
    D. the rotor bars are loose

20. Where constant speed is required, the one of the following motors that should be used is a

    A. wound-rotor motor B. series motor
    C. compound motor D. shunt motor

21. To reverse the direction of rotation of a 3-phase induction motor,

    A. the field connections should be reversed
    B. the armature connections should be reversed
    C. any two line leads should be interchanged
    D. the brushes should be shifted in the direction opposite to that of the armature rotation

22. The speed of a wound-rotor motor may be increased by

    A. *decreasing* the resistance in the secondary circuit
    B. *increasing* the resistance in the secondary circuit
    C. *decreasing* the shunt field current
    D. *increasing* the series field resistance

23. The one of the following methods which can be used to increase the slip of the rotor in a single-phase shaded-pole motor, is the

    A. reversal of the leads of the field winding
    B. addition of capacitors in series with the starting winding
    C. reduction of the impressed voltage
    D. addition of more capacitors in parallel with the starting winding

24. The direction of rotation of a single-phase A.C. repulsion motor may be reversed by

    A. interchanging the two line leads to the motor
    B. interchanging the leads to the main winding
    C. interchanging the leads to the starting winding
    D. moving the brushes to the other side of the neutral position

25. The torque developed by a D.C. series motor is

    A. *inversely proportional* to the square of the armature current
    B. *proportional* to the square of the armature current
    C. *proportional* to the armature current
    D. *inversely proportional* to the armature current

KEY (CORRECT ANSWERS)

1. A
2. C
3. D
4. C
5. D

6. D
7. B
8. D
9. D
10. A

11. B
12. C
13. C
14. C
15. A

16. B
17. D
18. B
19. B
20. D

21. C
22. A
23. C
24. D
25. B

TEST 2

DIRECTIONS: Each question or incomplete statement is followed by several suggested answers or completions. Select the one that BEST answers the question or completes the statement. *PRINT THE LETTER OF THE CORRECT ANSWER IN THE SPACE AT THE RIGHT.*

1. The one of the following which is MOST commonly used to clean a commutator is   1.____

    A. emery cloth
    B. graphite
    C. a smooth file
    D. fine-grit sandpaper

2. The type of motor which requires BOTH A.C. and D.C. for operation is the   2.____

    A. compound motor
    B. universal motor
    C. synchronous motor
    D. squirrel-cage motor

3. Compensators are used for starting large   3.____

    A. shunt motors
    B. series motors
    C. induction motors
    D. compound motors

4. The device MOST frequently used to correct low lagging power factor is a(n)   4.____

    A. solenoid
    B. induction regulator
    C. induction motor
    D. synchronous motor

5. Of the following motors, the one with the HIGHEST starting torque is the   5.____

    A. compound motor
    B. series motor
    C. shunt motor
    D. split phase motor

6. The approximate efficiency of a 60-cycle, 6-pole induction motor running at 1050 rpm and having a synchronous speed of 1200 rpm, is   6.____

    A. 67.0%   B. 78.5%   C. 87.5%   D. 90.0%

7. The MAIN contributing factor to motor starter failures *usually* is   7.____

    A. overloading
    B. dirt
    C. bearing trouble
    D. friction

8. The neutral or grounded conductors in branch circuit wiring must be identified by being colored   8.____

    A. black or brown
    B. black with white traces
    C. white with black traces
    D. white or natural gray

9. The SMALLEST radius for the inner edge of any field bend in a 1-inch rigid or flexible conduit when type R wire is being used, is   9.____

    A. 3 inches   B. 5 inches   C. 6 inches   D. 10 inches

10. Thermal cutouts used to protect a motor against overloads may have a current rating of not more than   10.____

    A. the starting current of the motor
    B. 125% of the full-load current rating of the motor

C. the full-load current of the motor
D. the current-carrying capacity of the branch circuit conductors

11. The MAXIMUM size of EMT permitted is

    A. 4 inches   B. 3 1/2 inches   C. 3 inches   D. 2 inches

12. The type of equipment which is defined as a set of conductors originating at the load side of the service equipment and supplying the main and/or one or more secondary distribution centers, is a

    A. sub-feeder   B. feeder   C. main   D. service cable

13. The SMALLEST size rigid conduit that may be used in wiring is

    A. 3/8 inch   B. 1/2 inch   C. 3/4 inch   D. 1 inch

14. An enclosed 600-volt cartridge fuse must be of the knife-blade contact type if its ampere rating is

    A. 20   B. 40   C. 60   D. 80

15. An insulated ground for fixed equipment should be color coded

    A. yellow
    B. green or green with a yellow stripe
    C. blue or blue with a yellow stripe
    D. black

16. Of the following, the meter that CANNOT be used to measure A.C. voltage is the

    A. electrodynamic voltmeter
    B. electrostatic voltmeter
    C. D'Arsonval voltmeter
    D. thermocouple voltmeter

17. Of the following, an instrument frequently used to measure high insulation resistance is a(n)

    A. tong-test ammeter
    B. megger
    C. ohmmeter
    D. electrostatic voltmeter

18. When using a voltmeter in testing an electric circuit, the voltmeter should be placed in

    A. *series* with the circuit
    B. *parallel* with the circuit
    C. *parallel* or in *series* with a current transformer, depending on the current
    D. *series* with the active element

19. The MINIMUM number of wattmeters necessary to measure the power in the load of a balanced 3-phase, 4-wire system, is

    A. 1   B. 2   C. 3   D. 4

20. An instrument that measures electrical energy is the

    A. current transformer
    B. watthour meter
    C. dynamometer
    D. wattmeter

21. The one of the following items which can be used to *properly* test an armature for a   21.____
    shorted coil is a

    A. neon light   B. megger
    C. growler   D. pair of series test lamps

22. The instrument that measures loads at the load terminals, averaged over specified time   22.____
    periods, is the

    A. coulomb meter   B. wattmeter
    C. demand meter   D. var-hour meter

23. A multiplier is usually used to increase the range of   23.____

    A. voltmeter   B. watthour meter
    C. wheatstont bridge   D. Nernst bridge

24. The instrument used to indicate the phase relation between the voltage and the current   24.____
    of an A.C. circuit is called a

    A. power factor meter B. synchroscope
    C. phase indicator   D. var-hour meter

25. Except where busways are entering or leaving service or distribution equipment, the bot- 25.____
    tom of the busway enclosure for all horizontal busway runs should be kept at a MINIMUM
    height above the floor of

    A. 4 feet   B. 6 feet   C. 8 feet   D. 10 feet

KEY (CORRECT ANSWERS)

1.	D	11.	D
2.	C	12.	B
3.	C	13.	B
4.	D	14.	D
5.	B	15.	B
6.	C	16.	C
7.	B	17.	B
8.	D	18.	B
9.	C	19.	A
10.	B	20.	B

21. C
22. C
23. A
24. A
25. C

TEST 3

DIRECTIONS: Each question or incomplete statement is followed by several suggested answers or completions. Select the one that BEST answers the question or completes the statement. *PRINT THE LETTER OF THE CORRECT ANSWER IN THE SPACE AT THE RIGHT.*

1. The lubricant *commonly* used to make it **easier** to pull braid-covered cable into a duct is

    A. soapstone
    B. soft soap
    C. heavy grease
    D. light oil

2. Of the following, the conductor insulation which may be used in **wet** locations is type

    A. RH   B. RHH   C. RHW   D. RUH

3. Assume that at a certain distribution point you notice that among several of the conductors entering the same raceway, some have a half-inch band of yellow tape, while the others do not. The conductors with the yellow tape are all

    A. grounded   B. ungrounded   C. A.C.   D. D.C.

4. Conductors of the same length, same circular mil area and type of insulation, may be run in multiple

    A. under no circumstances
    B. if each conductor is #4 or larger
    C. if each conductor is #2 or larger
    D. if each conductor is #1/0 or larger

5. In order to keep conduits parallel where several parallel runs of conduit of varying size are installed through 45 or 90 degree bends, it is BEST to

    A. bend conduit on the job
    B. use standard factory-made elbows
    C. use flexible connectors to adjust runs
    D. bend conduit at the factory

6. The BEST way to join two lengths of conduit which cannot be turned is to

    A. use a split adapter
    B. use a conduit union ("Erickson")
    C. cut running threads on one end of one length of the conduit
    D. cut running threads on the ends of both lengths of conduit

7. When an electrical splice is wrapped with both rubber tape and friction tape, the MAIN purpose of the friction tape is to

    A. protect the rubber tape
    B. provide additional insulation
    C. build up the insulation to the required thickness
    D. increase the strength of the splice

8. Assume that explosion-proof wiring is required in a certain area. Conduits entering an enclosure in this area which contains apparatus that may produce arcs, sparks or high temperature, should be provided with

   A. a cable terminator
   B. an approved sealing compound
   C. couplings with three full threads engaged
   D. insulated bushings

8.____

9. If installed in dry locations, wireways may be used for circuits of not more than

   A. 208 volts   B. 440 volts   C. 600 volts   D. 1100 volts

9.____

10. An interior wiring circuit has two conductors, one white and one black. Assume that it becomes necessary to add a third conductor as a switch leg. The color of the THIRD conductor should be

    A. blue   B. red   C. green   D. natural gray

10.____

11. Keyless lampholders rated at 1500 watts have bases which are classed as

    A. Intermediate   B. Medium   C. Mogul   D. Admedium

11.____

12. In precast cellular concrete floor raceways, the LARGEST conductor which may be installed, except by special permission, is

    A. No. 2   B. No. 0   C. No. 00   D. No. 000

12.____

13. The conductor insulation which may be used for fixture wire is type

    A. TF   B. TW   C. TA   D. RW

13.____

14. Multiple fuses are permissible

    A. under no circumstances
    B. for conductors longer than 1/0
    C. for conductors larger than 2/0
    D. for conductors larger than 4/0

14.____

15. In loosening a nut, a socket wrench with a ratchet handle should be used in preference to other types of wrenches if

    A. the nut is out of reach
    B. the turning space for the handle is limited
    C. the nut is worn
    D. greater leverage is required

15.____

16. Solders used for electrical connections are alloys of

    A. tin and lead   B. tin and zinc
    C. lead and zinc   D. tin and copper

16.____

17. Another name for a pipe wrench is a

    A. crescent wrench   B. torque wrench
    C. Stillson wrench   D. monkey wrench

17.____

18. The tool used to cut raceways is a hacksaw with fine teeth, *commonly* called a

    A. crosscut saw
    B. keyhole saw
    C. rip saw
    D. tube saw

19. Lead expansion anchors are MOST commonly used to fasten conduit to a

    A. wooden partition wall
    B. plaster wall
    C. solid concrete wall
    D. gypsum wall

20. The use of "running" threads when coupling two sections of conduit is

    A. always good practice
    B. good practice only when installing enameled conduit
    C. good practice only if it is impossible to turn one of the conduits
    D. always poor practice

21. A quick-break knifeswitch is often used rather than a standard knifeswitch of the same rating because the quick-break knife switch

    A. resists burning due to arcing at the contact points
    B. is easier to install and align
    C. is simpler in construction
    D. can carry a higher current without over-heating

22. The tip of a soldering iron is made of copper because

    A. copper is a very good conductor of heat
    B. solder will not stick to other metals
    C. it is the cheapest metal available
    D. the melting point of copper is very high

23. Good practice requires that cartridge fuses be removed from their clips by using a fuse puller rather than the bare hand. The reason for using the fuse puller is that the

    A. bare hand may be burned or otherwise injured
    B. fuse is less likely to break
    C. fuse clips may be damaged when pulled
    D. use of the bare hands slows down removal of fuse and causes arcing

24. The frame of a portable electric tool should be grounded in order to

    A. reduce leakage from the winding
    B. prevent short circuits
    C. reduce the danger of overheating
    D. prevent the frame from becoming alive to ground

25. The LEAST desirable device for measuring the dimensions of an electrical equipment cabinet containing live equipment, is a

    A. wooden yardstick
    B. six-foot folding wooden ruler
    C. twelve-inch plastic ruler
    D. six-foot steel tape

KEY (CORRECT ANSWERS)

1. A
2. C
3. D
4. D
5. A

6. B
7. A
8. B
9. C
10. B

11. C
12. B
13. A
14. A
15. B

16. A
17. C
18. D
19. C
20. D

21. A
22. A
23. A
24. D
25. D

TEST 4

DIRECTIONS: Each question or incomplete statement is followed by several suggested answers or completions. Select the one that BEST answers the question or completes the statement. *PRINT THE LETTER OF THE CORRECT ANSWER IN THE SPACE AT THE RIGHT.*

1. If three equal resistance coils are connected in parallel, the resistance of this combination is **equal to** 1.__

    A. one-third the resistance of one coil
    B. the resistance of one coil
    C. three times the resistance of one coil
    D. nine times the resistance of one coil

2. The voltage to neutral of a 3-phase, 4-wire system, is 120 volts. The line-to-line voltage is 2.__

    A. 208 volts   B. 220 volts   C. 230 volts   D. **240 volts**

3. Three 6-ohm resistances are connected in Y across a 3-phase circuit. If a current of 10 amperes flows through each resistance, the TOTAL power in watts drawn by this load is, *most nearly,* 3.__

    A. 600   B. 1200   C. 1800   D. 2400

4. A conduit in an outlet box should be provided with a locknut 4.__

    A. on the outside and bushing on the inside
    B. and bushing on the inside
    C. on the inside and bushing on the outside
    D. and bushing on the inside

5. If the current in a single-phase, 120-volt circuit is 10 amperes and a wattmeter in this circuit reads 1080 watts, the power factor is, *most nearly,* 5.__

    A. 1.11   B. .9   C. .8   D. .7

6. It is poor practice to use a file without a handle because the 6.__

    A. file may be dropped and damaged
    B. unprotected end may mar the surface being filed
    C. user may be injured
    D. file marks will be too deep

7. If a 60-cycle, 4-pole squirrel-cage, induction motor has a slip of 5%, its speed is, *most nearly,* 7.__

    A. 1800 rpm   B. 1795 rpm   C. 1750 rpm   D. 1710 rpm

8. The PROPER way to reverse the direction of rotation of a 3-phase wound rotor induction motor is to 8.__

    A. reverse two leads between the rotor and the control resistances
    B. shift the brushes
    C. reverse two supply leads
    D. open one rotor lead

9. Sulphuric acid should **always** be poured into the water when new electrolyte for a lead-acid battery is prepared. The reason for this precaution is to

   A. *avoid* splattering of the acid
   B. *avoid* explosive fumes
   C. *prevent* corrosion of the mixing vessel
   D. *prevent* clotting of the acid

10. The direction of rotation of a d.c. shunt motor can be reversed PROPERLY by

    A. reversing the two supply leads
    B. shifting the position of the brushes
    C. reversing the connections to both the armature and the field
    D. reversing the connections to the field

Questions 11-13.

DIRECTIONS: Questions 11 to 13, inclusive, refer to this excerpt from the electrical code on the subject of grounding electrodes.

Each buried plate electrode shall present not less than two square feet of surface to the exterior soil. Electrodes of plate copper shall be at least .06 inch in thickness. Electrodes of iron or steel plate shall be at least one-quarter inch in thickness. Electrodes of iron or steel pipe shall be galvanized and not less than three-quarter inch in internal diameter. Electrodes of rods of steel or iron shall be at least three-quarter inch minimum cross-section dimension... Driven electrodes of pipes or rods... shall be driven to a depth of at least eight feet regardless of the size or number of electrodes used... Each electrode used shall be separated at least six feet from any other electrode including those used for signal circuits, radio, lightning rods or any other purposes.

11. According to the above paragraph, all grounding electrodes MUST be

    A. of plate copper
    B. of iron pipe
    C. at least three-quarter inch minimum cross-section dimension
    D. separated at least six feet from any other electrode

12. According to the above paragraph, the one of the following electrodes which meets the code requirements is a(n)

    A. copper plate 12" X 18" X .06"
    B. steel plate 14" X 24" X .06"
    C. copper plate 12" X 24" X .06"
    D. iron plate 12" X 18" X .25'"

13. According to the above paragraph, the one of the following electrodes which meets the code requirements is

    A. plain iron pipe, 1" in internal diameter, driven to a depth of 10 feet
    B. galvanized iron pipe, 3/4" in internal diameter, driven to a depth of 6 feet
    C. plain steel pipe, 1" in internal diameter, driven to a depth of 7 feet
    D. galvanized steel pipe, 3/4" in internal diameter, driven to a depth of 9 feet

14. With reference to armature windings, lap windings are often called

    A. ring windings B. multiple windings
    C. series windings D. toroidal windings

15. The question refers to the diagram below.

    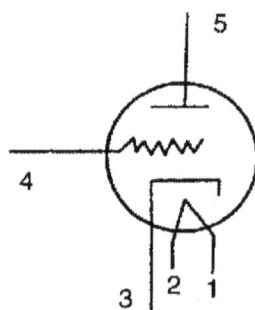

    The element numbered 4 is usually called the

    A. plate B. grid C. filament D. cathode

16. To properly mount an outlet box on a concrete ceiling, it is BEST to use

    A. expansion screw anchors B. wooden plugs
    C. wood screws D. masonry nails

17. A d.c. motor takes 30 amps, at 110 volts and has an efficiency of 90%. The horsepower available at the pulley is, *approximately*,

    A. 5 B. 4 C. 3 D. 2

18. If the armature current drawn by a series motor doubles, the torque

    A. remains the same B. doubles
    C. becomes 4 times as great D. becomes 8 times as great

19. The full load current, in amperes, of a 110-volt, 10 H.P., d.c. motor having an efficiency of 80% is, *approximately*,

    A. 62 B. 85 C. 99 D. 133

Questions 20-21.

DIRECTIONS: Questions 21 and 22 are to be answered in accordance with the diagram below.

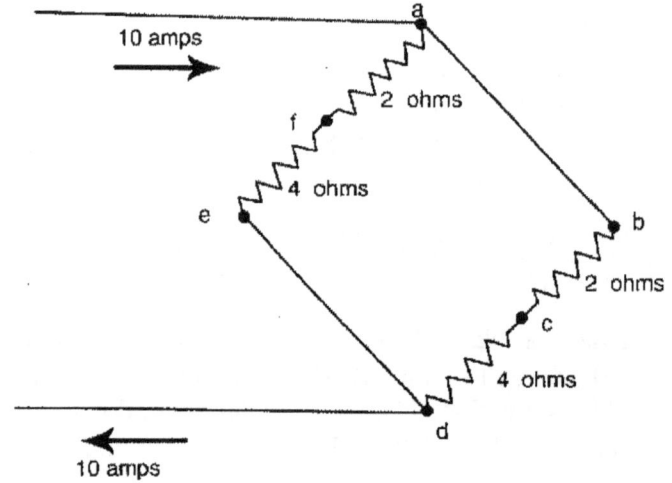

20. With reference to the above diagram, the voltage difference between points c and f is, most nearly,

   A. 40 volts   B. 20 volts   C. 10 volts   D. 0 volts

21. With reference to the above diagram, the current flowing through the resistance c d is, most nearly,

   A. 10 amperes   B. 5 amperes   C. 4 amperes   D. 2 amperes

Questions 22-25.

DIRECTIONS: Questions 22 through 25, inclusive, refer to the diagram below

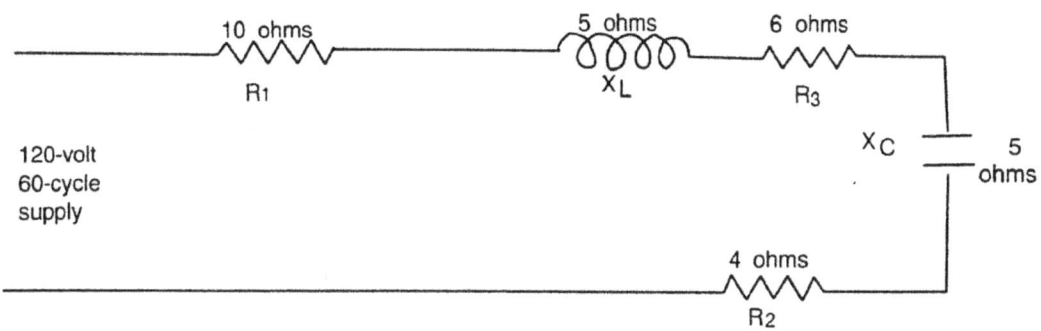

22. The value of the impedance in ohms of the above circuit is, most nearly,

   A. 60   B. 30   C. 25   D. 20

23. The current, in amperes, flowing in the above circuit is, most nearly,

   A. 2   B. 3   C. 6   D. 8

24. The potential drop, in volts, across R_3 is, most nearly,

   A. 12   B. 18   C. 36   D. 48

25. The power, in watts, consumed in the above circuit is, most nearly,

   A. 1080   B. 720   C. 180   D. 80

KEY (CORRECT ANSWERS)

1.	A	11.	D
2.	A	12.	C
3.	C	13.	D
4.	A	14.	B
5.	B	15.	B
6.	C	16.	A
7.	D	17.	B
8.	C	18.	C
9.	A	19.	B
10.	D	20.	D

21. B
22. D
23. C
24. C
25. B

———

TEST 5

DIRECTIONS: Each question or incomplete statement is followed by several suggested answers or completions. Select the one that BEST answers the question or completes the statement. *PRINT THE LETTER OF THE CORRECT ANSWER IN THE SPACE AT THE RIGHT.*

1. The heat dissipation, W, in a resistor having a resistance of R ohms connected across a supply of E volts, is proportional to E^2/R.
   If R is reduced to one-half of its former value and E is doubled, the heat dissipation in this resistor is *now*

   A. 8W B. 2W C. 4W D. 1/2W

2. Solder commonly used for electrical work is composed, *most likely*, of

   A. lead and tin B. antimony and zinc
   C. lead and zinc D. silver and antimony

3. A condenser having a capacitance of 3 microfarads is connected in parallel with a condenser having a capacitance of 2 microfarads. The combination is equal to a single condenser having a capacitance, in microfarads, of, *most nearly*,

   A. 5/6 B. 6/5 C. 5 D. 6

4. Of the following units, the one which is a unit of inductance is the

   A. maxwell B. henry C. weber D. oersted

5. The tool *commonly* used for bending conduit of small sizes is called a

   A. mandrel B. bending wrench C. hickey D. kinker

6. If a cartridge fuse clip makes contact with its fuse with much less than normal spring tension, the result would MOST likely be that the

   A. fuse will immediately burn out
   B. voltage at the supply will be high
   C. voltage at the load will be high
   D. clips will become warm

7. Of the following units, the one which is a unit of work or energy is the

   A. joule B. faraday C. coulomb D. farad

8. The one of the following substances which is the BEST conductor of electricity is

   A. iron B. aluminum C. tin D. copper

9. The formula for the resistance of one branch of a wye which is equivalent to a given delta is $R_a = \dfrac{A}{A+B+C}$.
   If $A = B = C = 3$, the value of R_a is, *most nearly*,

   A. 1 B. 3 C. 6 D. 9

10. When a splice is soldered, flux is used to

   A. act as a binder
   B. lubricate the surfaces
   C. keep the surfaces clean
   D. prevent rapid loss of heat

11. A 2000 ft. cable which has an insulation resistance of 180 megohms is cut in half. The insulation resistance of one of the 1000-ft. lengths will be, *most nearly,*

   A. 720 megohms
   B. 360 megohms
   C. 90 megohms
   D. 45 megohms

12. The area in circular mils of a piece of bare copper wire whose diameter is 0.1" is, *most nearly,*

   A. 780 B. 1,000 C. 7,800 D. 10,000

13. The resistance of a piece of copper wire is

   A. *directly* proportional to its diameter
   B. *inversely* proportional to its length
   C. *directly* proportional to the square of its diameter
   D. *inversely* proportional to its cross-sectional area

14. If an incandescent lamp is operated at a voltage which is higher than its rated voltage, the

   A. lumens output will be less than rated value
   B. current drawn will be less than rated value
   C. power consumed will be less than rated value
   D. life of the lamp will be less than rated value

15. The one of the following that is BEST suited to fight electrical fires is a

   A. CO_2 fire extinguisher
   B. soda-acid fire extinguisher
   C. foam fire extinguisher
   D. very fine spray of water

16. In order to get MAXIMUM power output from a battery, the external resistance should *equal*

   A. zero
   B. one-half of the internal resistance of the battery
   C. the internal resistance of the battery
   D. twice the internal resistance of the battery

17. A voltmeter with a scale range of 0-5 has a resistance of 500 ohms. The resistance, in ohms, of a multiplier for this instrument which will give it a range of 0 to 150 volts is, *most nearly,*

   A. 750 B. 2,500 C. 14,500 D. 75,000

18. The one of the following items which is *commonly* used to increase the range of a d.c. ammeter is a

   A. ceramicon
   B. shunt
   C. current transformer
   D. bridging transformer

19. Continuity of the conductors in an electrical circuit can be determined *conveniently* in the field by means of a(n)   19.____

    A. bell and battery set
    B. Maxwell bridge
    C. Preece test
    D. ammeter

Questions 20-25.

DIRECTIONS: Questions 20 to 25, inclusive, refer to the symbols of the A.S.A. which are listed below.

1.	(D)	6.	F⊃	11.	(W)	16.	⫼⫼⫼
2.	⊖	7.	▣	12.	WH	17.	(C)
3.	(F)	8.	S_2	13.	(B)	18.	⊏⊐
4.	⊙	9.	F	14.	⇝	19.	SC
5.	⊖$_3$	10.	▽	15.	P	20.	S_{mc}

20. A push button is designated by the symbol numbered   20.____

    A. 4   B. 7   C. 13   D. 15

21. A fire alarm station is designated by the symbol numbered   21.____

    A. 3   B. 6   C. 9   D. 10

22. A duplex convenience outlet is designated by the symbol numbered   22.____

    A. 1   B. 2   C. 5   D. 17

23. A battery is designated by the symbol numbered   23.____

    A. 10   B. 13   C. 16   D. 18

24. A double pole switch is designated by the symbol numbered   24.____

    A. 1   B. 2   C. 8   D. 15

25. The designation for a 3-wire circuit is numbered   25.____

    A. 3   B. 5   C. 11   D. 14

KEY (CORRECT ANSWERS)

1. A	11. B
2. A	12. D
3. C	13. D
4. B	14. D
5. C	15. A
6. D	16. C
7. A	17. C
8. D	18. B
9. A	19. A
10. C	20. B

21. C
22. B
23. C
24. C
25. D

TEST 6

DIRECTIONS: Each question or incomplete statement is followed by several suggested answers or completions. Select the one that BEST answers the question or completes the statement. *PRINT THE LETTER OF THE CORRECT ANSWER IN THE SPACE AT THE RIGHT.*

1. A good magnetic material is 1.____

   A. aluminum   B. iron   C. brass   D. carbon

2. A thermo-couple is a device for 2.____

   A. changing frequency
   B. changing d.c. to a.c.
   C. measuring temperature
   D. heat insulation

3. It is desired to operate a 6-volt lamp from a 120-volt a.c source. This can be done with the LEAST waste of power by using a 3.____

   A. series resistor
   B. rectifier
   C. step-down transformer
   D. rheostat

4. Rosin is a material *generally* used 4.____

   A. in batteries
   B. as a dielectric
   C. as a soldering flux
   D. for high voltage insulation

5. A milliampere is 5.____

   A. 1000 amperes
   B. 100 amperes
   C. .01 ampere
   D. .001 ampere

6. A compound motor usually has 6.____

   A. only a shunt field
   B. only a series field
   C. no brushes
   D. both a shunt and a series field

7. To connect a d.c. voltmeter to measure a voltage higher than the scale maximum, use a 7.____

   A. series resistance
   B. shunt
   C. current transformer
   D. voltage transformer

8. The voltage applied to the terminals of a storage battery to charge it CANNOT be 8.____

   A. rectified a.c.
   B. straight d.c.
   C. pulsating d.c.
   D. ordinary a.c.

9. When two unequal condensers are connected in parallel, the 9.____

   A. total capacity is decreased
   B. total capacity is increased
   C. result will be a short-circuit
   D. smaller one will break down

10. A megohm is 10.____

    A. 10 ohms
    B. 100 ohms
    C. 1000 ohms
    D. 1,000,000 ohms

11. Of the following, the poorest conductor of electricity is

   A. brass   B. lead   C. an acid solution   D. slate

12. A flashlight battery, a condenser, and a flashlight bulb are connected in series with each other. If the bulb burns brightly and steadily, then the condenser is

   A. open-circuited   B. short-circuited
   C. good   D. fully charged

13. A kilowatt of power will be taken from a 500-volt d.c. supply by a load of

   A. 200 amperes   B. 20 amperes   C. 2 amperes   D. 0.2 ampere

14. A commutator is used on a shunt generator in order to

   A. step-up voltage   B. step-up current
   C. change a.c. to d.c. D. control generator speed

15. The number of cells connected in series in a 6-volt storage battery of the lead-acid type is

   A. 2   B. 3   C. 4   D. 5

16. A 15-ampere circuit breaker as compared to a 15-ampere plug fuse

   A. can be reclosed   B. is cheaper
   C. is safer   D. is smaller

17. Lengths of rigid conduit are connected together to make up a long run by means of

   A. couplings   B. bushings   C. hickeys   D. lock nuts

18. BX is *commonly* used to indicate

   A. rigid conduit without wires
   B. flexible conduit without wires
   C. insulated wires covered with flexible steel armor
   D. insulated wires covered with a non-metallic covering

19. Good practice is to cut BX with a

   A. hacksaw   B. 3-wheel pipe cutter
   C. bolt cutter   D. heavy pliers

20. Silver is used for relay contacts in order to

   A. improve conductivity   B. avoid burning
   C. reduce costs   D. avoid arcing

21. Rigid conduit is fastened on the inside of the junction box by means of

   A. a bushing   B. a locknut
   C. a coupling   D. set-screw clamps

22. Of the following, the material which can BEST withstand high temperature is   22._____

    A. plastic   B. enamel   C. fiber   D. mica

23. A lead-acid type of storage battery exposed to freezing weather is *most likely* to freeze when the   23._____

    A. battery is fully charged   B. battery is complete discharged
    C. water level is low   D. cap vent holes are plugged

24. An important reason making it poor practice to put telephone wires in the same conduit with a.c. power lines is that   24._____

    A. power will be lost from the a.c. line
    B. the conduit will overheat
    C. the wires may be confused
    D. the telephone circuits will be noisy

25. In a loaded power circuit, it is MOST dangerous to   25._____

    A. *close* the circuit with a circuit breaker
    B. *close* the circuit with a knife switch
    C. *open* the circuit with a knife switch
    D. *open* the circuit with a circuit breaker

KEY (CORRECT ANSWERS)

1.	B	11.	D
2.	C	12.	B
3.	C	13.	C
4.	C	14.	C
5.	D	15.	B
6.	D	16.	A
7.	A	17.	A
8.	D	18.	C
9.	B	19.	A
10.	D	20.	A

21. A
22. D
23. B
24. D
25. C

TEST 7

DIRECTIONS: Each question or incomplete statement is followed by several suggested answers or completions. Select the one that BEST answers the question or completes the statement. *PRINT THE LETTER OF THE CORRECT ANSWER IN THE SPACE AT THE RIGHT.*

1. When fastening electrical equipment to a hollow tile wall, it is good practice to use   1.___
    A. toggle bolts
    B. wood screws
    C. nails
    D. ordinary bolts and nuts

2. Of the following, the MOST important reason for keeping the oil in a transformer tank moisture-free is to prevent   2.___
    A. rusting
    B. voltage breakdown
    C. freezing of the oil
    D. overheating

3. A voltmeter is generally connected to a high potential a.c. bus through a(n)   3.___
    A. auto-transformer
    B. potential transformer
    C. resistor
    D. relay

4. The HIGHEST total voltage which can be measured by using two identical 0-300 volt range d.c. meters connected in series would be   4.___
    A. 150 volts   B. 300 volts   C. 450 volts   D. 600 volts

5. Transistors are MAINLY employed in electrical circuits to take the place of   5.___
    A. resistors   B. condensers   C. inductances   D. vacuum tubes

6. The MINIMUM number of 10-ohm,1-ampere resistors which would be required to give an equivalent resistance of 10 ohms capable of carrying a 2-ampere load is   6.___
    A. 2   B. 3   C. 4   D. 5

7. To increase the current measuring range of an ammeter, the equipment *commonly* employed is a   7.___
    A. series resistor
    B. shunt
    C. short-circuiting switch
    D. choke

8. If a 10-watt lamp and a 100-watt lamp, each rated at 120 volts, are connected in series to a 240-volt source, then the voltage *across* the 10-watt lamp will be   8.___
    A. zero
    B. about 24 volts
    C. exactly 120 volts
    D. much more than 120 volts

9. If the load on the secondary of a small 10 to 1 step-up transformer is 100 watts, then the power being taken by the *primary* from the power line   9.___
    A. is less than 100 watts
    B. is exactly 100 watts
    C. is more than 100 watts
    D. may be more or less than 100 watts depending on the nature of the load

10. A 1/2-ohm, a 2-ohm, a 5-ohm, and a 25-ohm resistor are connected in series to a power source. The resistor which will consume the MOST power is the

   A. 1/2-ohm B. 2-ohm C. 5-ohm D. 25-ohm

10.____

11. With respect to 60-cycle current, it is CORRECT to say that one cycle takes

   A. 1/60th of a second B. 1/30th of a second
   C. 1/60th of a minute D. 1/30th of a minute

11.____

12. A rheostat is used in the field circuit of a shunt generator to control the

   A. generator speed B. load
   C. generator voltage D. power factor

12.____

13. If a condenser has a safe working voltage of 250 volts d.c. then it would be *most likely* to break down if used across a

   A. 250-volt,60-cycle a.c. line B. 250-volt d.c. line
   C. 240-volt battery D. 120-volt, 25-cycle a.c. line

13.____

14. Transformer cores are generally made up of thin steel lamin-ations. The MAIN purpose of this is to

   A. reduce the transformer losses
   B. reduce the initial cost of the transformer
   C. increase the weight of the transformer
   D. prevent voltage breakdown in the transformer

14.____

15. The MAIN reason for using copper tips in soldering irons is that copper

   A. is a good heat conductor B. is a good electrical conductor
   C. has a low melting point D. is very soft

15.____

16. Five identical electric fans, each rated at 120-volts d.c., are connected in series with each other on a 600-volt circuit. If one fan develops an open circuit, then

   A. the remaining fans will run, but at slow speed
   B. the remaining fans will run, but at above normal speed
   C. only one fan will run
   D. none of the fans will run

16.____

17. The pressure of a carbon brush on a commutator is measured with a

   A. spring balance B. feeler gage C. taper gage D. wire gage

17.____

18. A non-inductive carbon resistor consumes 50 watts when connect ted across a 120-volt d.c.source. If it is connected across a 120-volt a.c. source, the power consumed by the resistor will be nearest to

   A. 30 watts B. 40 watts C. 50 watts D. 60 watts

18.____

19. Of the following, the combination of lamps which will draw the MOST current from a standard 120-volt branch circuit is one with

   A. three 150-watt lamps B. one 300-watt lamp
   C. four 100-watt lamps D. six 50-watt lamps

19.____

20. A condenser is sometimes connected across contact points which make and break a d.c. circuit in order to reduce arcing of the points. The condenser produces this effect because it   20.___

    A. discharges when the contacts open
    B. charges when the contacts open
    C. charges while the contacts are closed
    D. discharges when the contacts are closed

KEY (CORRECT ANSWERS)

1.	A	11.	A
2.	B	12.	C
3.	B	13.	A
4.	D	14.	A
5.	D	15.	A
6.	C	16.	D
7.	B	17.	A
8.	D	18.	C
9.	C	19.	A
10.	D	20.	B

ELECTRICITY
EXAMINATION SECTION
TEST 1

DIRECTIONS: Each question or incomplete statement is followed by several suggested answers or completions. Select the one that BEST answers the question or completes the statement. *PRINT THE LETTER OF THE CORRECT ANSWER IN THE SPACE AT THE RIGHT.*

1. The electrical code requires that the controller for an A.C. motor shall be capable of interrupting 1.____

   A. twice the full load current of the motor
   B. three times the full load current of the motor
   C. five times the full load current of the motor
   D. the stalled rotor current

2. The MINIMUM number of overload devices required for a 3Ø A.G. motor connected to a 120/208 volt system is 2.____

   A. 1   B. 2   C. 3   D. 4

3. A feeder tap shall be considered as properly protected when the smaller conductors terminate in a single properly sized set of fuses or a circuit breaker, provided the 3.____

   A. tap is not over 25 feet long
   B. tap is not over 15 feet long
   C. current carrying capacity of the tap is at least 1/3 the rating of the fuse or circuit breaker protecting the main
   D. tap is not over 25 feet long and its current carrying capacity is at least 1/3 the rating of the fuse protecting the main

4. Branch circuit conductors supplying a motor shall have a current carrying capacity, in percentage of the full load current rating of the motor, of NOT less than 4.____

   A. 100%   B. 125%   C. 150%   D. 200%

5. The motor disconnecting means shall be located 5.____
   A. within 10 feet of the motor   B. within sight of the controller
   B. within 15 feet of the motor   C. where convenient

6. The motor disconnecting means shall have a continuous duty rating, in percentage of the name plate current rating of the motor, of AT LEAST 6.____

   A. 100%   B. 115%   C. 150%   D. 125%

7. An externally operable switch may be used as a starter for a motor not over 2 HP and not over 300 volts provided it has a rating of AT LEAST_____of the _____ current of the motor. 7.____

   A. 200%; stalled rotor   B. 200%; full load
   C. 115%; full load   D. 150%; stalled rotor

8. A single disconnecting means may serve a group of motors provided

   A. all motors are 1/2 HP or less
   B. all motors are within a short distance from each other
   C. all motors are located within a single room and within sight of the disconnecting means
   D. one-half of the motors are located within a single room and within sight of the disconnecting means

9. A single-throw knife switch should be mounted so that

   A. gravity tends to close it
   B. it is in a vertical position
   C. it is accessible only to qualified persons
   D. gravity tends to open it

10. For oil burner motors, the disconnecting means shall be placed

    A. on the oil burner
    B. at the entrance to the basement
    C. inside the oil burner room
    D. not necessary

11. The MAIN reason for grounding conduit is to prevent it from becoming

    A. corroded by electrolysis
    B. magnetized
    C. accidentally energized at a higher potential than ground
    D. a source of radio interference

12. Large wires or cables are to pulled through conduit where there are a number of bends. This operation may be made easier by applying to the surface of these wires or cables a limited quantity of

    A. soapstone or talc   B. oil
    C. grease   D. rosin

13. Assume that a poly-phase synchronous converter having a field splitting or sectionalizing switch and a series field diverter is to be started from the A.C. side. When starting from the A.C. side, the sectionalizing switch should be _____ and the diverter should be _____.

    A. closed; closed   B. closed; opened
    C. opened; closed   D. opened; opened

14. In the electrical trade, the tool USUALLY used for bending small size pipe is a

    A. pipe hickey   B. grooved sheave bender
    C. roller bender   D. pipe wrench

15. For supplying both motor and lighting load, the type of A.C. distribution system commonly used is _____ wire.

    A. 2Ø - 4   B. 1Ø - 3   C. 3Ø - 3   D. 3Ø - 4

16. A set of conductors originating at a distribution center other than the main distribution center, and supplying one or more branch circuit distribution centers, is known as

    A. subservice   B. main   C. subfeeder   D. feeder

17. A lighting distribution panel board is to be fed from a 1Ø 3-wire grounded neutral A.C. feeder.
    The MAXIMUM number of 2-wire branch circuits that this panel board may supply is

    A. 20   B. 36   C. 42   D. any number

18. The type of socket that must be used for a 500 watt incandescent lamp is _____ base.

    A. screw shell medium   B. mogul
    C. intermediate   D. candelabra

19. The number of quarter bends between conduit fitting or boxes including those at the fitting or box shall NOT exceed

    A. 2   B. 4   C. 6   D. 8

20. A grounding conductor for portable or fixed equipment shall be
    A. white   B. grey   C. green   D. black

21. One foot of a certain size of nichrome wire has a resistance of 2 ohms.
    To make a heating element for a 600 watt, 120 volt toaster, the number of feet required is
    A. 5   B. 10   C. 12   D. 24

22. Which of the following wires has the LARGEST current carrying capacity?

    A. Asbestos   B. Rubber
    C. Waxed cotton   D. Thermoplastic

23. According to the electrical code, the sum of the continuous rating of the load consuming apparatus connected to the system or part of the system is defined as the _____ load of the system.

    A. computed   B. connected   C. calculated   D. rated

24. When fuses are used as motor protection, they shall be placed in

    A. all ungrounded conductors
    B. all conductors
    C. all but one ungrounded conductor
    D. half of the ungrounded conductors

25. Except for circuits of a system having a grounded neutral having no conductor at more than 150 volts to ground, plug fuses shall not be used in circuits where the voltage EXCEEDS _____ volts.

   A. 110   B. 125   C. 150   D. 250

KEY (CORRECT ANSWERS)

1. D
2. B
3. D
4. B
5. B

6. B
7. B
8. C
9. D
10. B

11. C
12. A
13. D
14. A
15. D

16. C
17. C
18. B
19. B
20. C

21. C
22. A
23. B
24. A
25. B

TEST 2

DIRECTIONS: Each question or incomplete statement is followed by several suggested answers or completions. Select the one that BEST answers the question or completes the statement. *PRINT THE LETTER OF THE CORRECT ANSWER IN THE SPACE AT THE RIGHT.*

1. Collector wires for a crane are supported at 25 foot intervals. The MINIMUM wire size that may be used is #

    A. 2   B. 4   C. 6   D. 8

2. It is necessary to space insulating supports for main collector wires of a crane forty feet apart.
   The wires run on the same horizontal plane must be separated_____inches.

    A. 3   B. 6   C. 8   D. 12

3. A reverse phase relay is a device which is PRIMARILY used

    A. to reverse rotation of 3-phase induction motors
    B. to prevent accidental reversal of a polyphase motor
    C. to reverse the current in case one phase is reversed
    D. as an overload relay for 3-phase motors

4. A 3Ø motor used on a crane or a hoist

    A. will not start if one phase is not live
    B. will not start with all resistance inserted
    C. will not start if brake solenoid is energized
    D. may use a common return wire

5. A branch circuit feed for a crane motor that runs through a room where the temperature exceeds 167° F (75° C) shall be type

    A. R
    B. SB
    C. AF
    D. fire retarded

6. A common return is used to feed 2 – 3Ø crane motors. It shall be

    A. installed in rigid conduit
    B. type AVA
    C. not permitted
    D. individually bushed

7. Surgical operating rooms GENERALLY shall be considered_____hazardous location(s).

    A. Class I   B. Class II   C. Class III   D. not a

8. Electrical installations in garages, unless located at least four feet above the floor, shall be governed by the requirements for

    A. Class I
    B. Class II
    C. Class III
    D. General wiring

9. Portable extension light cords used in a garage shall NOT exceed _____ feet.

   A. 8   B. 15   C. 20   D. 40

10. An underground service to a private garage shall be
    A. lead-covered conductors in rigid conduit or other approved types buried 18" or more
    B. lead-covered conductors in rigid conduit buried 12"
    C. lead-covered conductors in E.M.T. buried 18"
    D. type R conductors in rigid conduit buried 18"

11. High tension conductors for a skeleton sign shall
    A. be insulated for 10,000 volts
    B. be insulated for 15,000 volts
    C. be insulated for 30,000 volts
    D. not be used

12. Emergency lighting in a theatre shall be controlled
    A. from the stage lighting control
    B. from the lobby
    C. by double pole switches
    D. from the operators booth

13. The MINIMUM size system grounding conductor shall be NOT less than #

    A. 16   B. 8   C. 4   D. 1/0

14. If you had a choice of connecting to one of the following grounding electrodes, you would use
    A. buried plates
    B. driven rod
    C. gas piping system
    D. continuous metallic underground active water piping system

15. Grounding electrodes other than water piping systems shall have a resistance to ground NOT exceeding _____ ohms.

    A. 0   B. 5   C. 25   D. infinity

16. A grounding conductor for portable or fixed equipment shall be

    A. white   B. grey   C. green   D. black

17. The MAXIMUM number of outlets allowed on a 20 ampere branch lighting circuit is

    A. 2   B. 8   C. 10   D. 20

18. The MAXIMUM number of mogul sockets that may be used on a 115 volt heavy duty lampholder branch circuit is

    A. 2   B. 8   C. 10   D. 20

19. The voltage drop in a 120 volt lighting circuit should be kept to a minimum and may NOT Exceed _____ volts.

   A. 120 B. 5.2 C. 3 D. 2.5

20. A wire 100 feet long is divided into two parts so that the ratio of their lengths is 4/1. The length of the longer piece is _____ feet.

   A. 10 B. 20 C. 40 D. 80

21. An effect caused by dissimilar metals is known as

   A. thermoelectric
   B. thermopile
   C. thermostatic
   D. thermionic

22. With the weight of water used as a base, the ratio of weight to other liquids is known as
   A. density
   B. specific gravity
   C. viscosity
   D. buoyancy

23. A utility company would supply a lighting and power load with _____ wire service.

   A. 1Ø -3 B. 2Ø -3 C. 3Ø -3 D. 3Ø -4

24. A ballast in a fluorescent fixture is used to

   A. reduce A.C. hum
   B. limit the current
   C. lower capacitor voltage
   D. eliminate cycle flicker

25. A fluorescent lamp being basically an A.C. lamp

   A. cannot be used D.C.
   B. may be made adaptable for D.C. by connecting a fixed resistor of the proper value in series with the line and auxiliary
   C. may be used for D.C. providing the operating voltage is the same as that required for A.C.
   D. can be used on D.C. only when available voltage is higher than that required for operation on A.C.

KEY (CORRECT ANSWERS)

1. C
2. D
3. B
4. A
5. B

6. C
7. A
8. A
9. D
10. A

11. B
12. B
13. B
14. D
15. C

16. C
17. D
18. C
19. B
20. D

21. A
22. B
23. D
24. B
25. B

TEST 3

DIRECTIONS: Each question or incomplete statement is followed by several suggested answers or completions. Select the one that BEST answers the question or completes the statement. *PRINT THE LETTER OF THE CORRECT ANSWER IN THE SPACE AT THE RIGHT.*

1. The MAXIMUM voltage to ground for elevator control pushbuttons is _____ volts. 1._____

   A. 120 B. 208 C. 300 D. 600

2. The MINIMUM size equipment grounding conductor for high tension vertical distribution transformer cases is # 2._____

   A. 10 B. 8 C. 000 D. 0000

3. Vertical conduits for high tension steel armored cable shall be supported by building construction at intervals NOT exceeding _____ feet and encased in _____ inches of concrete. 3._____

   A. 25; 2 B. 35; 2 C. 35; 3 D. 25; 3

4. The MINIMUM distance that shall be maintained between bare metal parts having a potential difference of 125 volts on panelboards is 4._____

   A. 3/4" B. 1" C. 1 1/4" D. 1 1/2"

5. The frequency of the current at a load, as compared to that of the generator, 5._____

   A. depends on the load
   B. is lower
   C. is higher
   D. is the same

6. The resistance to the flow of magnetic flux is known as 6._____

   A. permeance
   B. reluctance
   C. resistance
   D. reactance

7. A conductor cutting magnetic lines of force at the rate of 10^8 lines per second will generate 1 7._____

   A. ohm B. ampere C. watt D. volt

8. An inverse time delay relay will operate _____ current. 8._____

   A. slower, the greater the
   B. faster, the greater the
   C. faster, the smaller the
   D. at the same speed regardless of the amount of

9. A 120 volt system feeds an arc lamp that is to operate at 15 amps, at 62 volts. What resistance must be inserted in the line for PROPER operation? _____ ohms. 9._____

   A. .26 B. 3.86 C. 4.13 D. 8

10. If you reversed the line leads to a D.C. compound motor, it would

    A. stop
    B. reverse
    C. run in the same direction
    D. slow down

11. A D.C. generator has an EMF of 115 volts and an internal resistance of .07 ohms. What is the voltage at the load when it is delivering 50 amperes?

    A. 111.5   B. 115   C. 118.5   D. 120

12. The sockets allowed for a 500 watt incandescent lamp is

    A. candelabra
    B. intermediate
    C. medium
    D. mogul

13. A single circuit may be used to feed several small motors, providing the largest motor does NOT exceed _____ amps.

    A. 6   B. 10   C. 15   D. 20

14. A compensator is a device used with induction motors to

    A. compensate for electrical losses of the motor
    B. compensate for volt drop in the motor
    C. increase the starting torque of the motor
    D. decrease the line voltage at starting

15. A 2 HP 3-phase 220 volt squirrel cage motor would USUALLY be started by means of a(n)

    A. compensator
    B. 3 or 4 point starting box
    C. reduced voltage starter
    D. across the line starter

16. The type of starting and speed control equipment that would be used for a 50 HP wound rotor induction motor is

    A. with resistors connected in rotor circuit
    B. a 3 point starting box
    C. an autotransformer (compensator)
    D. an automatic primary resistor type of starter

17. In order to reverse rotation of a 3-phase squirrel cage induction motor, you would reverse

    A. any two line leads
    B. all line leads
    C. the brush leads
    D. starting winding leads

18. Reversing direction of rotation of a 3∅ wound rotor motor could be done by reversing _____ leads.

    A. all slip-ring   B. all line   C. two slip-ring   D. two line

19. To change direction of rotation of a 4-wire 2-phase motor, 19._____

    A. interchange the leads of one phase
    B. interchange the leads of both phases
    C. reverse the leads from the slip rings
    D. do nothing, it cannot be readily reversed

20. In selecting a reversing type motor starter, for maximum protection, you would choose one that is 20._____

    A. separately controlled
    B. mechanically and electrically interlocked
    C. electrically interlocked
    D. mechanically interlocked

21. A 3Ø wound rotor motor running at full speed suddenly drops to half speed. The PROBABLE cause is 21._____

    A. the stator field is shorted
    B. a rotor winding shorted due to centrifugal force
    C. a rotor lead disconnected due to centrifugal force
    D. two rotor leads rubbing against each other

22. Of the following types of motors, the one that requires both A.C. and D.C. for operation is the motor. 22._____

    A. universal   B. compound
    C. squirrel cage   D. synchronous

23. If the D.C. field of a synchronous motor is overexcited, 23._____

    A. it will run faster
    B. it will run slower
    C. line current will be leading
    D. it will hunt

24. A starter used for a synchronous motor would be 24._____

    A. an autotransformer   B. a resistor
    C. a rotor starter   D. the star-delta type

25. A 3Ø squirrel cage motor has 12 leads because 25._____

    A. it is a 6-phase motor
    B. they are stator and rotor leads
    C. 2 parallel leads are used on each winding
    D. the windings are used in parallel or series

KEY (CORRECT ANSWERS)

1.	C	11.	A
2.	D	12.	D
3.	A	13.	A
4.	A	14.	D
5.	D	15.	D
6.	B	16.	A
7.	D	17.	A
8.	B	18.	D
9.	B	19.	A
10.	C	20.	B

21. C
22. D
23. C
24. A
25. D

———

TEST 4

DIRECTIONS: Each question or incomplete statement is followed by several suggested answers or completions. Select the one that BEST answers the question or completes the statement. *PRINT THE LETTER OF THE CORRECT ANSWER IN THE SPACE AT THE RIGHT.*

1. To reverse direction of rotation of a split-phase motor, you would

    A. do nothing as it cannot be done
    B. reverse the line leads
    C. reverse polarity of all windings
    D. reverse polarity of starting winding

    1._____

2. To reverse a capacitor motor, you would reverse

    A. both auxiliary and main windings
    B. the line leads
    C. the condenser
    D. the auxiliary winding

    2._____

3. In a capacitor motor, the condenser is connected

    A. in series with the field
    B. across the motor terminals
    C. in parallel with the starting winding
    D. in series with the starting winding

    3._____

4. To reverse the direction of a repulsion-induction motor, you should

    A. move the brushes so they cross the pole axis
    B. interchange terminal connections
    C. reverse the starting winding
    D. change the connections to the armature

    4._____

5. To reverse rotation of a shaded pole motor, you would

    A. reverse the armature leads
    B. reverse the field leads
    C. shift the brushes
    D. do nothing as the motor cannot be readily reversed

    5._____

6. A split-phase motor runs hot at no load.
   The probable reason is the
    A. starting winding is open
    B. starting winding is reversed
    C. centrifugal switch is broken
    D. running winding is completely shorted

    6._____

39

7. The difference between the operating speed and the synchronous speed of an induction machine is called the

   A. slip   B. phase   C. acceleration   D. frequency

8. The speed, in R.P.M., of a 10-pole, 60 cycle, 3ø alternator is MOST NEARLY

   A. 3600   B. 4800   C. 1440   D. 720

9. A 2300 volt 80% PF, 60 cycle, 8-pole synchronous motor may be DIRECTLY connected to a pump designed for a speed of _____ RPM.

   A. 600   B. 900   C. 1200   D. 1800

10. The rated speed of a three-phase, 4-pole squirrel cage, 60 cycle motor is MOST NEARLY_____RPM.

    A. 900   B. 1200   C. 1750   D. 1800

11. The synchronous speed of a 4-pole, 25 cycle motor is

    A. 750 RPM   B. 375 RPM   C. 3750 RPM   D. not fixed

12. Three and four way switches are connected

    A. in series with the line
    B. across the line
    C. to the neutral
    D. only loads less than 5 amps

13. Travelers are distinguished by being

    A. not connected to a current consuming device
    B. connected to one hot line
    C. connected to a current consuming device
    D. connected to a grounded line

14. Of the following types of single phase induction motors, the one that produces the HIGHEST starting torque is by the _____ method.

    A. shaded pole
    B. repulsion start
    C. resistance split phase
    D. capacitor split phase

15. The break down torque will vary on a squirrel cage induction motor with a given slip _____ the voltage.

    A. inversely with
    B. with the square of
    C. with the
    D. with the square root of

16. A 95% efficient transformer supplies a 114 KW load. The input is_____ KW.

    A. 5.7   B. 108   C. 114   D. 120

17. A D.C. motor that takes 40 amperes at 250 volts delivers 10 horsepower. 17._____
    The efficiency of this motor is APPROXIMATELY

    A. 55%   B. 64%   C. 75%   D. 100%

18. A 5 HP 220 volt D.C. motor that has an efficiency of 90% takes a full load current of 18._____
    APPROXIMATELY_____ amps.

    A. 143   B. 17   C. 18.8   D. 20.5

19. A 20 HP D.C. motor is 85% efficient. 19._____
    The power, in kilowatts, that it will take from the line is

    A. 12.7   B. 17.5   C. 20.0   D. 23.5

20. The current taken by a 1 HP 120 volt single-phase induction motor whose efficiency is 20._____
    90% and power factor of 0.8 is _____amps.
    A. 6.9   B. 7.8   C. 8.6   D. 6.2

21. If electricity costs 3¢ per KWH, what is the cost of running a 440 volt 3Ø 10 HP motor 21._____
    whose efficiency is 80% for one hour?

    A. 3¢   B. 18¢   C. 22¢   D. 28¢

22. Three motor control start-stop pushbutton stations are connected 22._____
    A. in series   B. in parallel
    C. three way   D. in series-parallel

23. The torque of a D.C. shunt motor varies as the _____ 23._____
    A. armature current
    B. cube of armature current
    C. field current squared
    D. square of the armature current

24. For fast stopping, a braking method sometimes utilizes a motor as a generator to create 24._____
    a retarding force.
    This method is known as

    A. magnetic braking   B. dynamic braking
    C. counter EMF braking   D. plugging

25. An instrument used to measure the angular speed of a motor is the 25._____
    A. tachometer   B. micrometer
    C. monometer   D. speedometer

KEY (CORRECT ANSWERS)

1. D
2. D
3. D
4. A
5. D

6. C
7. A
8. D
9. B
10. C

11. A
12. A
13. A
14. A
15. B

16. D
17. C
18. C
19. B
20. C

21. D
22. D
23. A
24. B
25. A

TEST 5

DIRECTIONS: Each question or incomplete statement is followed by several suggested answers or completions. Select the one that BEST answers the question or completes the statement. *PRINT THE LETTER OF THE CORRECT ANSWER IN THE SPACE AT THE RIGHT.*

1. Interpoles are

    A. connected in series with the shunt field
    B. connected in parallel with the armature
    C. used to increase the degree of compounding
    D. used to improve commutation

2. In the D.C. shunt motor, the field

    A. has comparatively few turns of wire
    B. has comparatively many turns of wire
    C. is connected in series with the armature
    D. current is more than the line current

3. If, in a compound motor, the series and shunt fields oppose each other, the motor

    A. is differential compound
    B. is cumulative compound
    C. will not run
    D. will overheat

4. A cumulative compound motor has _____ set(s) of fields.

    A. 1   B. 2   C. 3   D. 4

5. To reverse rotation of a D.C. shunt motor, you would

    A. reverse the line leads
    B. reverse the series fields
    C. reverse the armature connections
    D. shift the brushes

6. The PROPER way to reverse the direction of rotation of a compound motor is to interchange the

    A. line leads   B. armature connections
    C. shunt field connections   D. series field connections

7. If you attempted to start a D.C. compound motor in which the series field was open-circuited, the motor would

    A. not start   B. blow the fuse
    C. run away   D. start to reverse

8. If the field current of a shunt motor is decreased, the motor will

    A. run away   B. run slower
    C. run faster   D. overheat

43

9. To decrease the speed of a D.C. shunt wound motor below its name plate rating, it is advisable to connect

   A. resistance in the field circuit
   B. a shunt across the field circuit
   C. resistance in the armature circuit
   D. a shunt across the armature circuit

10. The reason for using a starting box for a D.C. motor is to

    A. reduce armature current during starting period
    B. increase the starting torque
    C. regulate the speed
    D. reduce voltage on fields during starting

11. The holding coil of a 3-point starting box is connected

    A. in series with the field
    B. in series with the line
    C. in series with the armature
    D. across the line

12. When replacing a D.C. blowout coil, it is MOST important to

    A. have its resistance the same as the old coil
    B. have its resistance higher than the old coil
    C. see that the magnetic field reacts
    D. install it when the contacts are open

13. The usual cause of localized heating of an armature is

    A. overload
    B. eddy currents
    C. armature out of center between poles
    D. shorted armature coil

14. What would happen when a D.C. motor is running with an open armature coil?

    A. Speed would increase.
    B. Speed would decrease.
    C. Motor would begin to spark violently.
    D. The coil would begin heating.

15. An electrical contractor files an application for inspection for a job
    A. when completed   B. when starting
    C. when half finished   D. before starting

16. Polarizing a fixture means

    A. attaching the fixture to the outlet box
    B. connecting identified conductor to shell of lampholder
    C. removing the insulation from the fixture wires
    D. connecting unidentified conductor to shell of lamp-holder

3 (#5)

17. A closed circuit burglar alarm system is better than an open circuit system because   17._____

    A. it costs less to install
    B. it gives greater protection
    C. the bell will not ring if the wire is cut
    D. it requires fewer parts

18. A portable electric drill should be grounded by means of   18._____

    A. standard attachment plug
    B. 3-prong attachment plug
    C. T slot attachment plug
    D. cord connector

19. A single pole switch is ALWAYS connected in the   19._____

    A. neutral leg   B. white wire
    C. identified wire   D. live leg

20. The SAFEST way for an electrician to determine whether a circuit is A.C. or D.C. is to   20._____

    A. use a neon test lamp
    B. test bare parts with his fingertips
    C. telephone the Edison Company
    D. use an incandescent test lamp

21. Which of the following is NOT permitted for permanent wiring in New York City?   21._____

    A. Armored cable (BX)   B. Rigid conduit
    C. Romex   D. EMT

22. In rigid conduit work, the GREATEST number of quarter bends (90°) permitted between outlets is   22._____

    A. two   B. four   C. six   D. eight

23. The standard network system used for light and power in New York City is   23._____

    A. 110/220 volt single phase
    B. 220 volt 2 phase 3 wire
    C. 208/120 volt 3 phase 4 wire
    D. 120/240 volt single phase 3 wire

24. The SMALLEST size service entrance conductor permitted is   24._____

    A. #2   B. #4   C. #6   D. #8

25. The ampere rating of service switches must be AT LEAST _____ amperes.   25._____

    A. 60   B. 30   C. 200   D. 100

KEY (CORRECT ANSWERS)

1. D
2. B
3. A
4. B
5. C

6. B
7. A
8. C
9. C
10. A

11. A
12. D
13. D
14. C
15. D

16. B
17. B
18. B
19. C
20. A

21. C
22. B
23. C
24. A
25. D

EXAMINATION SECTION
TEST 1

DIRECTIONS: Each question or incomplete statement is followed by several suggested answers or completions. Select the one that BEST answers the question or completes the statement. *PRINT THE LETTER OF THE CORRECT ANSWER IN THE SPACE AT THE RIGHT.*

Questions 1-6.

DIRECTIONS: Questions 1 through 6 are to be answered on the basis of the circuit diagram below. All switches are initially open.

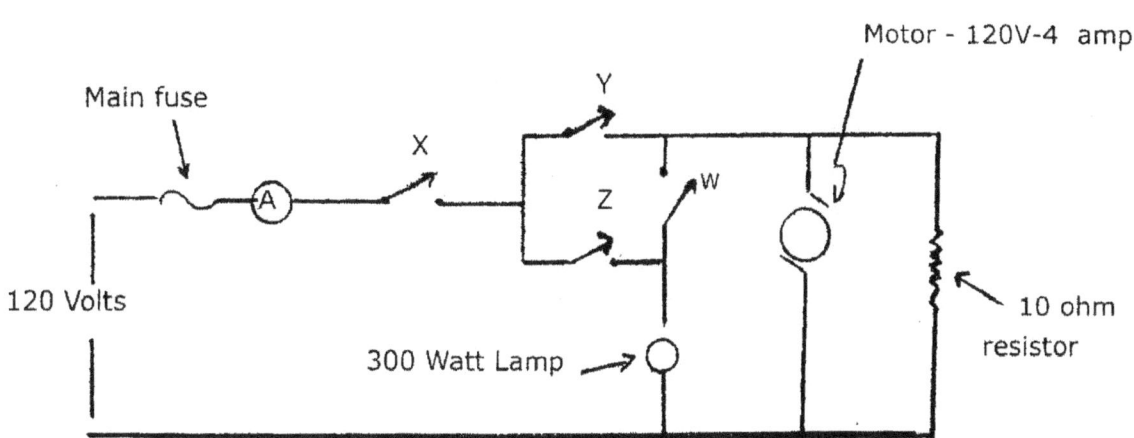

1. To light the 300 watt lamp, the following switches MUST be closed: 1.____

   A. X and Y   B. Y and Z   C. X and Z   D. X and W

2. If all of the switches W, X, Y, and Z are closed, the following will happen: 2.____

   A. The lamp will light and the motor will rotate
   B. The lamp will light and the motor will not rotate
   C. The lamp will not light and the motor will not rotate
   D. A short circuit will occur and the main fuse will blow

3. With 120 volts applied across the 10 ohm resistor, the current drawn by the resistor is _____ amp(s). 3.____

   A. 1/12   B. 1.2   C. 12   D. 1200

4. With 120 volts applied to the 10 ohm resistor, the power used by the resistor is _____ kw. 4.____

   A. 1.44   B. 1.2   C. .144   D. .12

5. The current drawn by the 300 watt lamp when lighted should be APPROXIMATELY _____ amps. 5.____

   A. 2.5   B. 3.6   C. 25   D. 36

47

6. In the circuit shown, the symbol A is used to indicate a (n)

   A. ammeter
   B. *and* circuit
   C. voltmeter
   D. wattmeter

7. Of the following materials, the BEST conductor of electricity is

   A. iron   B. copper   C. aluminum   D. glass

8. The sum of 6'6", 5'9", and 2' 1 1/2" is

   A. 13'4 1/2"   B. 13'6 1/2"   C. 14'4 1/2"   D. 14'6 1/2"

9.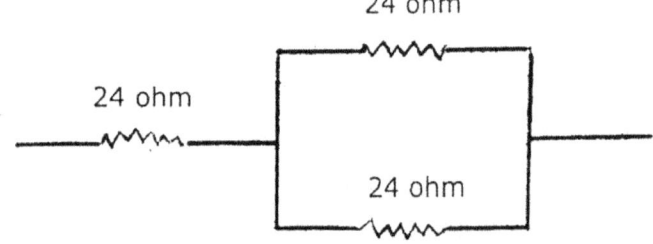

   The equivalent resistance of the three resistors shown in the sketch above is _____ ohms.

   A. 8   B. 24   C. 36   D. 72

10.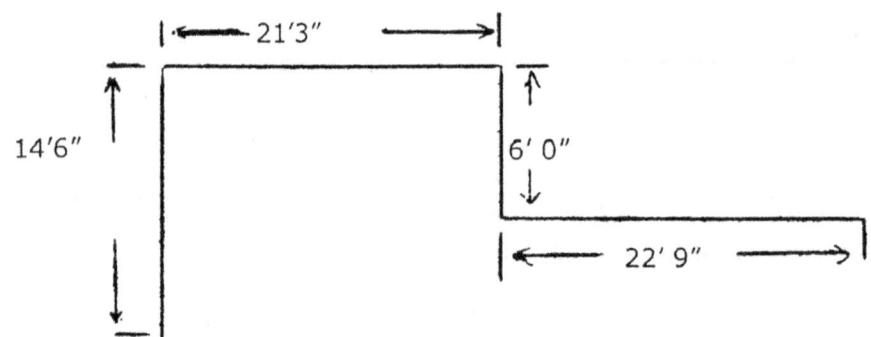

    The TOTAL length of electrical conduit that must be run along the path shown on the diagram above is

    A. 63'8"   B. 64'6"   C. 65'6"   D. 66'8"

11. Of the following electrical devices, the one that is NOT normally used in direct current electrical circuits is a (n)

    A. circuit breaker
    B. double-pole switch
    C. transformer
    D. inverter

12. The number of 120-volt light bulbs that should NORMALLY be connected in series across a 600-volt electric line is

    A. 1   B. 2   C. 3   D. 5

13. Of the following motors, the one that does NOT have any brushes is the _____ motor. 13.____

    A. d.c. shunt
    B. d.c. series
    C. squirrel cage induction
    D. compound

14. Of the following materials, the one that is COMMONLY used as an electric heating element in an electric heater is 14.____

    A. zinc
    B. brass
    C. terne plate
    D. nichrome

Questions 15-25.

DIRECTIONS: Questions 15 through 25 are to be answered on the basis of the instruments listed below. Each instrument is listed with an identifying number in front of it.

    1 - Hygrometer
    2 - Ammeter
    3 - Voltmeter
    4 - Wattmeter
    5 - Megger
    6 - Oscilloscope
    7 - Frequency meter
    8 - Micrometer
    9 - Vernier caliper
    10 - Wire gage
    11 - 6-foot folding rule
    12 - Architect's scale
    13 - Planimeter
    14 - Engineer's scale
    15 - Ohmmeter

15. The instrument that should be used to accurately measure the resistance of a 4,700 ohm resistor is Number 15.____

    A. 3   B. 4   C. 7   D. 15

16. To measure the current in an electrical circuit, the instrument that should be used is Number 16.____

    A. 2   B. 7   C. 8   D. 15

17. To measure the insulation resistance of a rubber-covered electrical cable, the instrument that should be used is Number 17.____

    A. 4   B. 5   C. 8   D. 15

18. An AC motor is hooked up to a power distribution box.
    In order to check the voltage at the motor terminals, the instrument that should be used is Number 18.____

    A. 2   B. 3   C. 4   D. 7

19. To measure the shaft diameter of a motor accurately to one-thousandth of an inch, the instrument that should be used is Number 19.____

    A. 8   B. 10   C. 11   D. 14

20. The instrument that should be used to determine whether 25 Hz. or 60 Hz. is present in an electrical circuit is Number 20.____

    A. 4   B. 5   C. 7   D. 8

21. Of the following, the PROPER instrument to use to determine the diameter of the conductor of a piece of electrical hook-up wire is Number

    A. 10   B. 11   C. 12   D. 14

22. The amount of electrical power being used in a balanced three-phase circuit should be measured with Number

    A. 2   B. 3   C. 4   D. 5

23. The electrical wave form at a given point in an electronic circuit can be observed with Number

    A. 2   B. 3   C. 6   D. 7

24. The PROPER instrument to use for measuring the width of a door is Number

    A. 11   B. 12   C. 13   D. 14

25. A one-inch hole with a tolerance of plus or minus three-thousandths is reamed in a steel block.
    The PROPER instrument to use to accurately check the diameter of the hole is Number

    A. 8   B. 9   C. 11   D. 14

KEY (CORRECT ANSWERS)

1. C
2. A
3. C
4. A
5. A

6. A
7. B
8. C
9. C
10. B

11. C
12. D
13. C
14. D
15. D

16. A
17. B
18. B
19. A
20. C

21. A
22. C
23. C
24. A
25. B

TEST 2

DIRECTIONS: Each question or incomplete statement is followed by several suggested answers or completions. Select the one that BEST answers the question or completes the statement. *PRINT THE LETTER OF THE CORRECT ANSWER IN THE SPACE AT THE RIGHT.*

1. The number of conductors required to connect a 3-phase delta connected heater bank to an electric power panel board is

   A. 2   B. 3   C. 4   D. 5

   1.____

2. Of the following, the wire size that is MOST commonly used for branch lighting circuits in homes is _____ A.W.G.

   A. #12   B. #8   C. #6   D. #4

   2.____

3. When installing electrical circuits, the tool that should be used to pull wire through a conduit is a

   A. mandrel
   B. snake
   C. rod
   D. pulling iron

   3.____

4. Of the following AC voltages, the LOWEST voltage that a neon test lamp can detect is _____ volts.

   A. 6   B. 12   C. 80   D. 120

   4.____

5. Of the following, the BEST procedure to use when storing tools that are subject to rusting is to

   A. apply a thin coating of soap onto the tools
   B. apply a light coating of oil to the tools
   C. wrap the tools in clean cheesecloth
   D. place the tools in a covered container

   5.____

6. If a 3 1/2 inch long nail is required to nail wood framing members together, the nail size to use should be

   A. 2d   B. 4d   C. 16d   D. 60d

   6.____

7. Of the four motors listed below, the one that can operate only on alternating current is a(n) _____ motor.

   A. series
   B. shunt
   C. compound
   D. induction

   7.____

8. The sum of 1/3 + 2/5 + 5/6 is

   A. 1 17/30   B. 1 3/5   C. 1 15/24   D. 1 5/6

   8.____

9. Of the following instruments, the one that should be used to measure the state of charge of a lead-acid storage battery is a(n)

   A. ammeter
   B. ohmmeter
   C. hydrometer
   D. thermometer

   9.____

51

10. If three 1 1/2 volt dry cell batteries are wired in series, the TOTAL voltage provided by the three batteries is _____ volts.

   A. 1.5   B. 3   C. 4.5   D. 6.0

11. Taking into account time and one-half payment for time over 40 hours of work, the gross pay of an employee who works 43 hours in a week at a rate of pay of $10.68 per hour is

   A. $427.20   B. $459.24   C. $475.26   D. $491.28

12. The sum of 0.365 + 3.941 + 10.676 + 0.784 is

   A. 13.766   B. 15.666   C. 15.756   D. 15.766

13. In order to transmit mechanical power between two rotating shafts at right angles to each other, two gears are used. Of the following, the type of gears that should be used are _____ gears.

   A. herringbone   B. spur
   C. bevel   D. rack and pinion

14. To properly ground the service electrical equipment in a building, a ground connection should be made to _____ the building.

   A. the waste or soil line leaving
   B. the vent line going to the exterior of
   C. any steel beam in
   D. the cold water line entering

15. The area of the triangle shown at the right is _____ square inches.
   A. 120
   B. 240
   C. 360
   D. 480

Questions 16-25.

DIRECTIONS: Questions 16 through 25 are to be answered on the basis of the tools shown on the next page. The tools are not shown to scale. Each tool is shown with an identifying number alongside it.

3 (#2)

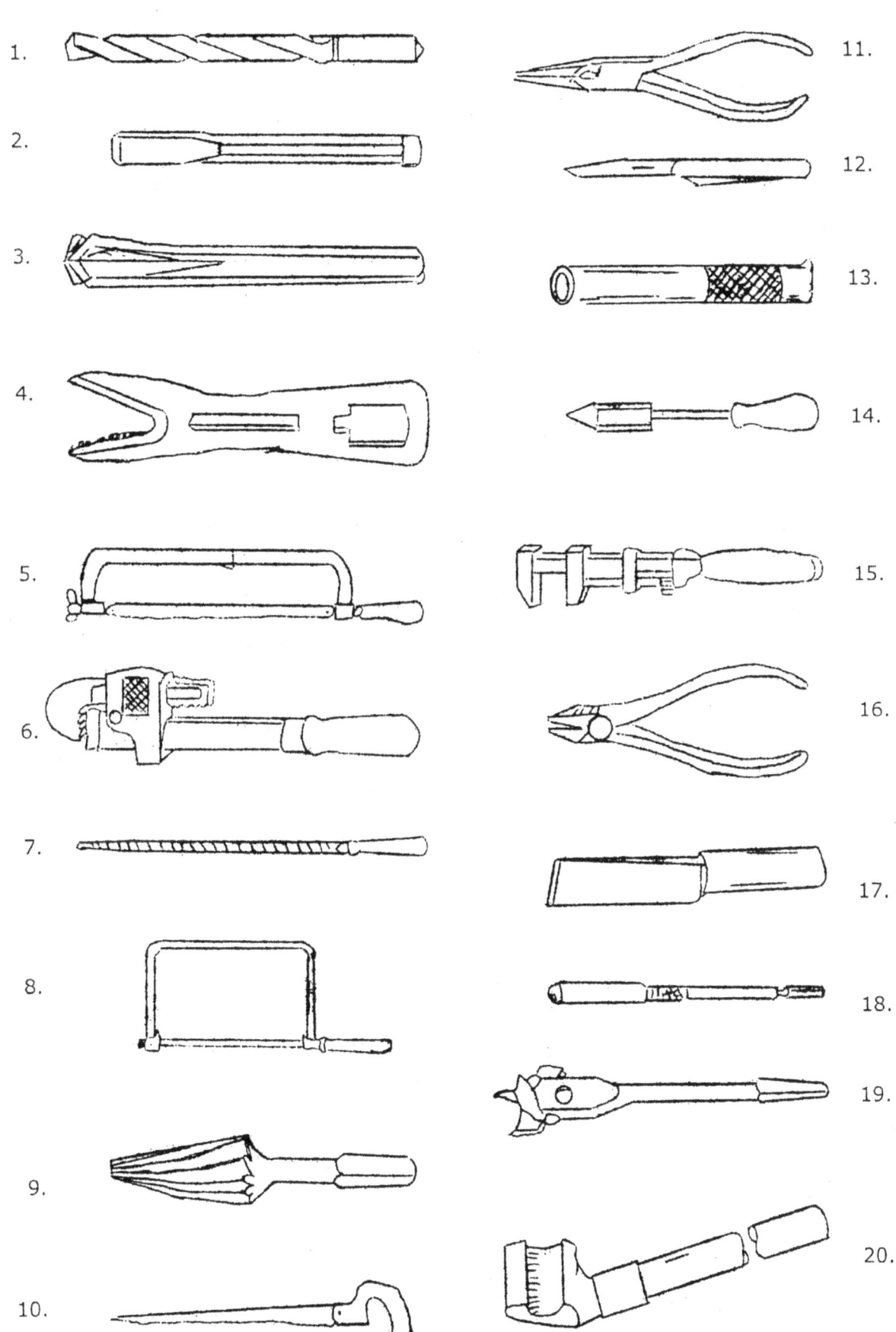

16. The tool that should be used for cutting thin wall steel conduit is Number 16.____

    A. 5 B. 8 C. 10 D. 16

17. The tool that should be used for cutting a 1 7/8 inch diameter hole in a wood joist is Number 17.____

    A. 3 B. 9 C. 14 D. 19

18. The tool that should be used for soldering splices in electrical wire is Number 18.____

    A. 3 B. 7 C. 13 D. 14

19. After cutting off a piece of 3/4 inch diameter electrical conduit, the tool that should be used for removing a burr from the inside of the conduit is Number 19.____

    A. 9 B. 11 C. 12 D. 14

20. The tool that should be used for turning a coupling onto a threaded conduit is Number 20.____

    A. 6 B. 11 C. 15 D. 16

21. The tool that should be used for cutting wood lathing in plaster walls is Number 21.____

    A. 5 B. 7 C. 10 D. 12

22. The tool that should be used for drilling a 3/8 inch diameter hole in a steel beam is Number 22.____

    A. 1 B. 2 C. 3 D. 9

23. Of the following, the BEST tool to use for stripping insulation from electrical hook-up wire is Number 23.____

    A. 11 B. 12 C. 15 D. 20

24. The tool that should be used for bending an electrical wire around a terminal post is Number 24.____

    A. 4 B. 11 C. 15 D. 16

25. The tool that should be used for cutting electrical hookup wire is Number 25.____

    A. 5 B. 12 C. 16 D. 17

KEY (CORRECT ANSWERS)

1. B
2. A
3. B
4. C
5. B

6. C
7. D
8. A
9. C
10. C

11. C
12. D
13. C
14. D
15. A

16. A
17. D
18. D
19. A
20. A

21. C
22. A
23. B
24. B
25. C

TEST 3

DIRECTIONS: Each question or incomplete statement is followed by several suggested answers or completions. Select the one that BEST answers the question or completes the statement. *PRINT THE LETTER OF THE CORRECT ANSWER IN THE SPACE AT THE RIGHT.*

1. An electric circuit has current flowing through it. The panel board switch feeding the circuit is opened, causing arcing across the switch contacts.
   Generally, this arcing is caused by

   A. a lack of energy storage in the circuit
   B. electrical energy stored by a capacitor
   C. electrical energy stored by a resistor
   D. magnetic energy induced by an inductance

2. MOST filter capacitors in radios have a capacity rating given in

   A. microvolts   B. milliamps
   C. millihenries   D. microfarads

3. Of the following, the electrical wire size that is COMMONLY used for telephone circuits is _____ A.W.G.

   A. #6   B. #10   C. #12   D. #22

Questions 4-9.

DIRECTIONS: Questions 4 through 9 are to be answered on the basis of the electrical circuit diagram shown below, where letters are used to identify various circuit components.

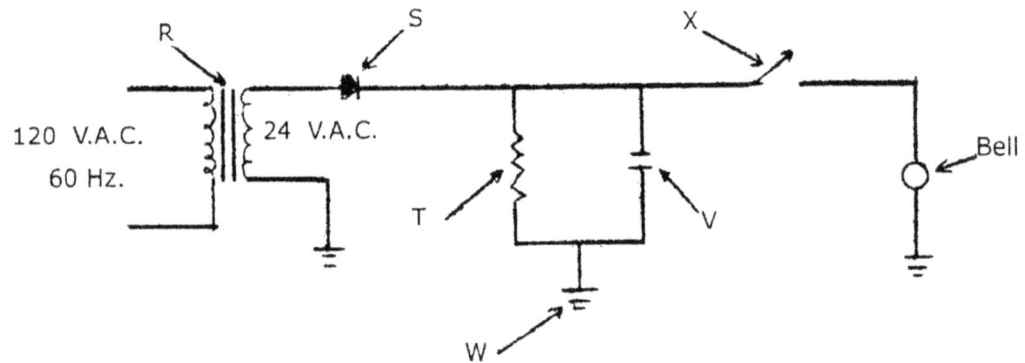

4. The device indicated by the letter R is a

   A. capacitor   B. converter
   C. resistor   D. transformer

5. The device indicated by the letter S is a

   A. transistor   B. diode
   C. thermistor   D. directional relay

56

6. The devices indicated by the letters T and V are used together to _____ components of the secondary current.

    A. reduce the AC
    B. reduce the DC
    C. transform the AC
    D. invert the AC

7. The letter W points to a standard electrical symbol for a

    A. wire
    B. ground
    C. terminal
    D. lightning arrestor

8. Closing switch X will apply the following type of voltage to the bell:

    A. 60 Hz. AC
    B. DC
    C. pulsating AC
    D. 120 Hz. AC

9. The circuit shown contains a _____ rectifier.

    A. mercury-arc
    B. full-wave
    C. bridge
    D. half-wave

10. A bolt specified as 1/4-28 means the following:
    The

    A. bolt is 1/4 inch in diameter and has 28 threads per inch
    B. bolt is 1/4 inch in diameter and is 2.8 inches long
    C. bolt is 1/4 inch long and has 28 threads
    D. threaded portion of the bolt is 1/4 inch long and has 28 threads per inch

11. When cutting 0.045-inch thickness sheet metal, it is BEST to use a hacksaw blade that has _____ teeth per inch.

    A. 7
    B. 12
    C. 18
    D. 32

12. To accurately tighten a bolt to 28 foot-pounds, it is BEST to use a(n) _____ wrench.

    A. pipe
    B. open end
    C. box
    D. torque

13. When bending a 2-inch diameter conduit, the CORRECT tool to use is a

    A. hickey
    B. pipe wrench
    C. hydraulic bender
    D. stock and die

14. When soldering two #20 A.W.G. copper wires together to form a splice, the solder that SHOULD be used is _____ solder.

    A. acid-core
    B. solid-core
    C. rosin-core
    D. liquid

15. A bathroom heating unit draws 10 amperes at 115 volts.
    The hot resistance of the heating unit should be _____ ohms.

    A. .08
    B. 8
    C. 11.5
    D. 1150

16. Of the following materials, the one that is NOT suitable as an electrical insulator is

    A. glass
    B. mica
    C. rubber
    D. platinum

17. An air conditioning unit is rated at 1000 watts. The unit is run for 10 hours per day, five days per week.
If the cost for electrical energy is 5 cents per kilowatt-hour, the weekly cost for electricity should be

    A. 25¢   B. 50¢   C. $2.50   D. $25.00

17.____

18. If a fuse is protecting the circuit of a 15 ohm electric heater and it is designed to blow out at a current exceeding 10 amperes, the MAXIMUM voltage from among the following that should be applied across the terminals of the heater is _____ volts.

    A. 110   B. 120   C. 160   D. 600

18.____

19. Before opening a pneumatic hose connection, it is important to remove pressure from the hose line PRIMARILY to avoid

    A. losing air
    B. personal injury
    C. damage to the hose connection
    D. a build-up of pressure in the air compressor

19.____

20. If the scale on a shop drawing is 1/4 inch to the foot, then a part which measures 3 3/8 inches long on the drawing has an ACTUAL length of _____ feet _____ inches.

    A. 12; 6   B. 13; 6   C. 13; 9   D. 14; 9

20.____

21. The function that is USUALLY performed by a motor controller is to

    A. start and stop a motor
    B. protect a motor from a short circuit
    C. prevent bearing failure of a motor
    D. control the brush wear in a motor

21.____

22. Of the following galvanized sheet metal electrical outlet boxes, the one that is NOT a commonly used size is the _____ box.

    A. 4" square   B. 4" octagonal
    C. 4" x 2 1/8"   D. 4" x 1"

22.____

23. When soldering a transistor into a circuit, it is MOST important to protect the transistor from

    A. the application of an excess of rosin flux
    B. excessive heat
    C. the application of an excess of solder
    D. too much pressure

23.____

24. When installing BX type cable, it is important to protect the wires in the cable from the cut ends of the armored sheath.
The APPROVED method of providing this protection is to

    A. use a fiber or plastic insulating bushing
    B. file the cut ends of the sheath smooth
    C. use a connector where the cable enters a junction box
    D. tie the wires into an Underwriter's knot

24.____

25. While lifting a heavy piece of equipment off the floor, a person should NOT 25.____

   A. twist his body
   B. grasp it firmly
   C. maintain a solid footing on the ground
   D. bend his knees

26. It is important that metal cabinets and panels that house electrical equipment should be grounded PRIMARILY in order to 26.____

   A. prevent short circuits from occurring
   B. keep all circuits at ground potential
   C. minimize shock hazards
   D. reduce the effects of electrolytic corrosion

27. A foreman explains a technical procedure to a new employee. If the employee does not understand the instructions he has received, it would be BEST if he were to 27.____

   A. follow the procedure as best he could
   B. ask the foreman to explain it to him again
   C. avoid following the procedure
   D. ask the foreman to give him other work

28. Of the following, the BEST connectors to use when mounting an electrical panel box directly onto a concrete wall are 28.____

   A. threaded studs   B. machine screws
   C. lag screws   D. expansion bolts

29. Of the following, the BEST instrument to use to measure the small gap between relay contacts is 29.____

   A. a micrometer   B. a feeler gage
   C. inside calipers   D. a plug gage

30. A POSSIBLE result of mounting a 40 ampere fuse in a fuse box for a circuit requiring a 20 ampere fuse is that the 40 ampere fuse may 30.____

   A. provide twice as much protection to the circuit from overloads
   B. blow more easily than the smaller fuse due to an overload
   C. cause serious damage to the circuit from an overload
   D. reduce power consumption in the circuit

KEY (CORRECT ANSWERS)

1.	D	16.	D
2.	D	17.	C
3.	D	18.	B
4.	D	19.	B
5.	B	20.	B
6.	A	21.	A
7.	B	22.	D
8.	B	23.	B
9.	D	24.	A
10.	A	25.	A
11.	D	26.	C
12.	D	27.	B
13.	C	28.	D
14.	C	29.	B
15.	C	30.	C

EXAMINATION SECTION
TEST 1

DIRECTIONS: Each question or incomplete statement is followed by several suggested answers or completions. Select the one that BEST answers the question or completes the statement. *PRINT THE LETTER OF THE CORRECT ANSWER IN THE SPACE AT THE RIGHT.*

1. Two or more elevator cars can be coordinated so that each answers its own car calls and all hall calls coming from a given portion of the building.
   This type of operation is known as

   A. zoning
   B. group dispatching
   C. on-call service
   D. zone-space operation

   1._____

2. The MOST important reason for posting a Certificate of Inspection in an elevator is to

   A. instruct passengers to stand clear of the door
   B. inform passengers of the number of persons permitted to ride in the car
   C. prevent crowding at the car door
   D. assure the elevator mechanic that the elevator is in proper operating condition

   2._____

3. Elevator *buffers* are designed to

   A. bring the car and counterweights to a smooth stop
   B. prevent the elevator doors from jamming
   C. prevent the elevator cars from shaking sideways
   D. separate one elevator from another

   3._____

4. *Zoning* is used during periods of

   A. extremely light up or down peak traffic
   B. extremely heavy up or down peak traffic
   C. up peak service operation only
   D. down peak service operation only

   4._____

5. If a fully loaded car always skips floor calls during peak periods of traffic, the MOST likely cause is

   A. automatic by-pass of the floors
   B. a weak or faulty cable
   C. a misfunction in the call-button system
   D. improper wiring of the control panel

   5._____

6. Elevator *buffers* are located

   A. in the motor room
   B. on the top of the elevator car
   C. in the elevator pit
   D. on the car guard rails

   6._____

7. That portion of a floor, balcony, or platform used to receive and discharge passengers or freight is usually known as the elevator _____ zone.

   A. landing   B. leveling   C. service   D. operating

   7._____

8. A device which, when operated, will prevent the elevator from making a registered landing stop is called a

    A. non-stop switch
    B. governor
    C. limit switch
    D. gravity switch

9. All of the following are safety devices EXCEPT

    A. a governor
    B. a limit switch
    C. the interlocks
    D. a selector switch

10. The load-weighing device for automatic cars is located

    A. in the car pit
    B. beneath the elevator car platform
    C. in the control panel
    D. in the elevator mechanic's room

11. The MAIN purpose of the load-weighing device of an automatic elevator is to

    A. prevent operation of a crowded car
    B. speed up service
    C. keep the weight of the elevator constant
    D. open the door when an elevator is becoming overloaded

12. A device which is designed to prevent the movement of an automatic elevator car until the hoistway doors are mechanically locked in the closed position is known as the

    A. electronic switch
    B. interlock
    C. brake drum
    D. door-detector

13. The MAIN purpose of the photo-electric tube system in an elevator is to

    A. protect passengers
    B. assure a level landing
    C. prevent excessive speed
    D. control passenger load

14. The lights on the panelboard which show at which landings and for which direction elevator hall stop-or-signal calls are registered but unanswered are usually known as the _____ indicators.

    A. waiting passenger
    B. car position
    C. hall position
    D. landing

15. A cable made up of electric conductors, which provides electrical connections between an elevator car and a fixed outlet in the hoistway is known as the _____ cable.

    A. BX
    B. signal-transfer
    C. traveling
    D. registering

16. The devices mounted on the leading edges of the car doors to stop and reopen the doors if they touch a person or object are called

    A. safety shoes
    B. photo-electric rays
    C. door buffers
    D. emergency stop switches

17. If an elevator begins to overspeed, the device which is designed to open a safety switch and cut off power to the hoisting machine is the

    A. governor
    B. fuse
    C. controller
    D. speed limit interlock

18. *Peak-service operation* is a term usually used to describe an operation in which

    A. cars are dispatched to favor service in the direction of heavy travel
    B. cars take all passengers from their floors to the lobby without intermediate stops
    C. cars in reserve are automatically returned to the bottom terminal
    D. the starter controls the movements and direction of the cars' travel

19. *Time-space operation* is a term usually used to describe an operation in which cars are dispatched

    A. in one direction to favor service in that direction
    B. continuously in both directions to serve all passengers in minimum time
    C. in the direction of heavy travel only
    D. from the upper terminal at proper intervals to suit traffic

20. *Automatic car operation* is a term usually used to describe an operation in which each elevator is *automatically*

    A. controlled to stop in response to the car or hall calls for service in its direction of travel
    B. controlled to bypass certain floors in order to prevent delay at the bottom terminal
    C. controlled to bypass all hall calls
    D. dispatched to the upper floors with a full load

21. The operation that prevents service delay by a passenger who blocks the elevator door is known as

    A. bucking
    B. door detecting
    C. nudging
    D. dodging

22. In a photo-electric tube system, restoration of the light rays indicates that the car entrance is clear and the

    A. doors will stay open until the light ray is interrupted by a passenger
    B. doors are allowed to close
    C. elevator is empty
    D. elevator is moving upward

23. The term *premature* in connection with elevator doors refers to doors

    A. opening before the car is level with the landing
    B. closing before passengers enter the car
    C. opening faster than normal
    D. closing unusually slowly

24. When a person signals for an elevator and the elevator skips his floor because it is already overcrowded, which of the following should automatically occur?
    The
    A. elevator completes discharging passengers and returns to pick up the call
    B. signal is transferred to the next available car
    C. starter dispatches another car to answer the call
    D. signal puts more elevators into service

25. The MAIN reason that an elevator starter should watch the loading of the elevators is to insure that
    A. passengers will enter the cars quickly
    B. the number of passengers entering the car does not exceed the number allowed
    C. complaints from the passengers can be heard
    D. the public will see the need for elevator starters

KEY (CORRECT ANSWERS)

1. C		11. B	
2. B		12. B	
3. A		13. A	
4. B		14. A	
5. A		15. C	
6. C		16. A	
7. A		17. A	
8. A		18. A	
9. D		19. B	
10. B		20. A	

21. C
22. B
23. A
24. B
25. B

TEST 2

DIRECTIONS: Each question or incomplete statement is followed by several suggested answers or completions. Select the one that BEST answers the question or completes the statement. *PRINT THE LETTER OF THE CORRECT ANSWER IN THE SPACE AT THE RIGHT.*

1. Assume that an elevator is stuck and an elevator starter has spoken with the passengers on the intercom in order to reassure them.
   Of the following, the BEST action for the starter to take *next* is to

   A. ask the passengers for their home telephone numbers
   B. call the elevator mechanic
   C. stand by to assist in the emergency
   D. notify offices in the building that some of their employees are stuck in the elevator

   1.____

2. Starters are instructed never to allow an elevator to be moved that is not functioning properly.
   The MAIN reason for this is to

   A. avoid vandalism
   B. make the passengers comfortable
   C. prevent accidents
   D. simplify the repairs to be made

   2.____

3. After a starter has opened the shaft door of a manually operating elevator to place the car into service, the NEXT action that he should take is to

   A. put the lights on
   B. start the generator
   C. check to see that the floor is clean
   D. check that the car is at the landing

   3.____

4. Assume that an elevator starter sees a man trip and fall down near the elevators on the main floor of the building. The starter immediately goes over to the man, who says that he has twisted his ankle and cannot get up.
   Of the following, the FIRST action the starter should take is to

   A. ignore the incident since it was not caused by the operation of the elevators
   B. assist the injured man to move to a quiet area on the main floor
   C. summon an ambulance and be prepared to direct the medical people to the injured man
   D. make out a detailed accident report

   4.____

5. Of the following, the BEST way for a starter to maintain safe conditions for both passengers and employees is to *always*

   A. wear his uniform
   B. look busy
   C. keep a good attendance record
   D. observe rules and regulations

   5.____

65

6. A starter sees a man who is holding a typewriter run from an elevator and out of the building.
   The MOST important thing for the starter to try to remember right after the incident is

   A. the date of the incident
   B. the make or brand of the typewriter
   C. which elevator car the man was riding
   D. what the man looked like

7. In most buildings, it is requested that mail bags be carried out of the elevators instead of being dragged out. Of the following, the BEST reason for this is to

   A. prevent damage to the floor
   B. prevent damage to car panels
   C. make sure that the mail bags do not take up too much room in the elevators
   D. make the mailmen move faster

8. Assume that the only elevator in a building is being repaired and has been shut down by the mechanic during his lunch hour. A commissioner comes in and wants to go up to his office quickly.
   The BEST thing for a starter to do in this situation is to

   A. open the elevator and take the commissioner to his office
   B. tell the commissioner that a second elevator should be installed
   C. tell the commissioner that the elevator is out of service and tell him that he can use the stairs
   D. call the mechanic's supervisor and ask if it is all right to take the commissioner to his office

9. A starter observes a passenger leaving an elevator car with an open container of coffee. The passenger spills some coffee in front of the car landing on the main floor. The starter should IMMEDIATELY

   A. look for a porter
   B. report it to the custodian
   C. clean it up himself
   D. shut the cars down

10. The rated capacity of an elevator is usually stated in terms of

    A. velocity
    B. horsepower
    C. acceleration
    D. pounds

11. A starter notices a boy defacing the marble walls in the main floor lobby entrance of a building.
    Of the following, the FIRST action the starter should take is to

    A. ignore the boy's actions
    B. report the incident to the custodian
    C. force the boy to clean it up
    D. ask the boy to stop

12. Of the following, the MOST important reason for a starter to plan work schedules for the elevator operators under his supervision is so that

    A. unexpected emergency situations can be properly handled
    B. essential operations will be adequately covered
    C. the operators will be satisfied that the work is spread out equally
    D. the operators will know their jobs better

13. New instructions concerning the operation of a freight car were given to an elevator starter by his supervisor. If the starter does not understand these instructions, he should

    A. ask his supervisor to explain the new instructions
    B. follow the old procedures in the operation of the freight car
    C. ask the operator of the freight elevator for assistance
    D. have the regular freight operator brief him on the operations

14. A passenger complains that the elevator door hit him lightly on closing. The BEST thing for the elevator starter to do is to

    A. ask the passenger to report the incident to the custodian
    B. tell the passenger not to hold the door open for such a long time
    C. check the door and the safety light ray to see that they are working properly
    D. take the elevator out of service

15. The MOST important reason for a starter to remove dirt from the door floor saddle slot is to

    A. prevent the doors from becoming dirty
    B. allow the doors to close properly
    C. prevent the doors from being damaged
    D. make the porters' jobs easier

16. An elevator operator was injured as a result of slipping on an oily floor. This type of accident was MOST likely caused by

    A. defective equipment
    B. the physical condition of the operator
    C. improperly installed flooring
    D. poor housekeeping

17. If a car is stuck and there are no passengers in the elevator, which of the following is TRUE?
    The

    A. car will automatically return to service
    B. car door will automatically open
    C. starter will not have to report the incident
    D. alarm bell will not ring

18. Which of the following is NOT a duty of an elevator starter?

    A. Answering inquiries made by the public
    B. Observing the performance of a new elevator operator

C. Guarding against potential hazards
D. Delivering personal messages

19. A starter should be familiar with the location and main functions of agencies in the building MAINLY because this would

    A. show the public that the starter knows the job
    B. help the starter in directing persons to the right offices
    C. show that the starter is well educated
    D. increase the use of the elevators

20. The MAIN reason for quickly having the lights fixed when they go out in an elevator is to

    A. save power
    B. avoid accidents
    C. make dust visible
    D. restore the current

21. A woman tells an elevator starter that she is having difficulty completing an application for a certain city program whose office is located in the building. The woman asks the starter to help her complete the application.
    Which of the following is the BEST action for the starter to take?

    A. Help the woman complete the application and at the same time continue to perform his regular duties
    B. Tell the woman to complete the form as best she can
    C. Direct the woman to the program's office in the building
    D. Tell the woman that it would be illegal to help her

22. Of the following, the situation in which an elevator starter would be MOST justified in calling the police is if a passenger

    A. argues loudly with another passenger
    B. refuses to enter an elevator
    C. uses physical force on another passenger
    D. insults the starter

23. Elevator starters are urged to be courteous to passengers MAINLY because courtesy helps to

    A. maintain elevator schedules
    B. prevent unexpected accidents from occurring
    C. promote good public relations
    D. increase the use of elevators

24. In making a written report of an accident in which someone was injured, which of the following items is it LEAST important for an elevator starter to include in the report?

    A. The location of the accident
    B. An opinion of the extent of the injury
    C. The name of the injured person
    D. The date of the accident

25. Of the following, the MOST important reason for having an elevator starter write a complete report of a passenger accident which occurred in an elevator is to

    A. prove that the starter is alert
    B. assist in preventing future accidents
    C. assist the attending physician
    D. show that the elevator is safe

25.____

KEY (CORRECT ANSWERS)

1.	B	11.	D
2.	C	12.	B
3.	D	13.	A
4.	C	14.	C
5.	D	15.	B
6.	D	16.	D
7.	A	17.	D
8.	C	18.	D
9.	C	19.	B
10.	D	20.	B

21.	C
22.	C
23.	C
24.	B
25.	B

TEST 3

DIRECTIONS: Each question or incomplete statement is followed by several suggested answers or completions. Select the one that BEST answers the question or completes the statement. *PRINT THE LETTER OF THE CORRECT ANSWER IN THE SPACE AT THE RIGHT.*

Questions 1-6.

DIRECTIONS: Questions 1 through 6 are to be answered ONLY on the basis of the information given in the Elevator Operators' Work Schedule shown below.

ELEVATOR OPERATORS' WORK SCHEDULE

Operator	Hours of Work	A.M. Relief Period	Lunch Hour	P.M. Relief Period
Anderson	8:30-4:30	10:20-10:30	12:00- 1:00	2:20-2:30
Carter	8:00-4:00	10:10-10:20	11:45-12:45	2:30-2:40
Daniels	9:00-5:00	10:20-10:30	12:30- 1:30	3:15-3:25
Grand	9:30-5:30	11:30-11:40	1:00- 2:00	4:05-4:15
Jones	7:45-3:45	9:45- 9:55	11:30-12:30	2:05-2:15
Lewis	9:45-5:45	11:40-11:50	1:15- 2:15	4:20-4:30
Nance	8:45-4:45	10:50-11:00	12:30- 1:30	3:05-3:15
Perkins	8:00-4:00	10:00-10:10	12:00- 1:00	2:40-2:50
Russo	7:45-3:45	9:30- 9:40	11:30-12:30	2:10-2:20
Smith	9:45-5:45	11:45-11:55	1:15- 2:15	4:05-4:15

1. The two operators who are on P.M. relief at the same time are

    A. Anderson and Daniels B. Carter and Perkins
    C. Jones and Russo D. Grand and Smith

2. Of the following, the two operators who have the same lunch hour are

    A. Anderson and Perkins B. Daniels and Russo
    C. Grand and Smith D. Nance and Russo

3. At 12:15, the number of operators on their lunch hour is

    A. 3 B. 4 C. 5 D. 6

4. The operator who has an A.M. relief period right after Perkins and a P.M. relief period right before Perkins is

    A. Russo B. Nance C. Daniels D. Carter

5. The number of operators who are scheduled to be working at 4:40 is
   A. 5   B. 6   C. 7   D. 8

6. According to the schedule, it is MOST correct to say that
   A. no operator has a relief period during the time that another operator has a lunch hour
   B. each operator has to wait an identical amount of time between the end of lunch and the beginning of P.M. relief period
   C. no operator has a relief period before 9:45 or after 4:00
   D. each operator is allowed a total of 1 hour and 20 minutes for lunch hour and relief periods

7. In which of the following situations concerning an elevator operator is it MOST important for the operator's supervisor, an elevator starter, to take immediate action? The operator('s)
   A. uniform is not clean
   B. closes the car doors before the elevator is loaded to capacity
   C. answers an inquiry made by one of the passengers
   D. ignores a safety rule

8. Of the following, the BEST way for an elevator starter to make sure that elevator operators are performing their duties *properly* is to
   A. check the condition of the elevators daily
   B. ask the operators to follow instructions
   C. order one operator to report any errors committed by the other operators
   D. observe the operators at work and see how well they function

9. Which of the following should be the FIRST step in training a newly-hired elevator operator?
   A. Correct the operator's errors
   B. Show the operator how to do the work
   C. Write a report describing the operator's performance
   D. Let the operator do the job himself

10. In an emergency situation, an elevator starter should speak _____ manner.
    A. in a hurried and tense
    B. clearly and in a calm
    C. slowly and in a rambling
    D. quickly and in an excited

11. Of the following, which is the BEST way for a starter to instruct operators in the use of a new procedure?
    A. Tell one operator to show the other operators how to follow the new procedure
    B. Pass around a description of the new procedure
    C. Explain and demonstrate the new procedure to the operators
    D. Post a description of the new procedure on a bulletin board

12. When training new employees, a supervisor should expect that they will

    A. not all learn at the same rate
    B. need less training than experienced employees
    C. learn faster if the supervisor does not observe them performing their work
    D. learn better if they are trained during lunch hours

13. When introducing a new elevator operator to the job, an elevator starter should

    A. tell the operator that the work is very difficult
    B. have the operator memorize all the job's duties and responsibilities before beginning work
    C. tell the operator that every mistake will be noted on the probation report
    D. assume that the operator wants to perform as well as possible

14. An elevator operator tells her supervisor, an elevator starter, that she is considering submitting a suggestion to the employee suggestion program. The operator's suggestion concerns a way of improving elevator service in the building and may require the starter to occasionally walk greater distances than at present.
    Of the following, the BEST thing for the starter to do is to

    A. ask the operator whether she would like to walk around more if she were to become a starter
    B. encourage the operator to submit her idea to the employee suggestion program
    C. ask the operator to omit the part which requires the starter to do more work before submitting the suggestion
    D. tell the operator that employee suggestions are usually ignored

15. Assume that the elevator operators in a certain building have submitted their choices for vacation periods.
    In making up a vacation schedule for these operators, it would be MOST desirable for an elevator starter to

    A. try to give the operators their first choices for vacation periods
    B. make sure that the best operators get their first choice before preparing the rest of the schedule
    C. draw up a schedule first and then see how it compares with the operators' choices
    D. assign earlier vacation periods to senior operators and later periods to newer operators

16. In planning the daily work schedules for the elevator operators in a building, it would be MOST desirable for an elevator starter to

    A. give all the operators the same lunch hour so that they will eat together
    B. give longer rest periods to operators who have more seniority
    C. make sure that there are enough operators on duty during periods of heavy traffic
    D. assign the least desirable working hours to the newer operators

17. Of the following, the FIRST time an elevator starter should tell a new elevator operator the basic safety rules of the job is

    A. during the operator's introduction to the job
    B. once passengers have complained about the operator's recklessness

C. after the operator has had a minor accident when operating the elevators
D. when the operator completes the probation period

18. Assume that a newly hired elevator operator has been operating an elevator for two weeks.
Of the following, which is the BEST method for the operator's supervisor, an elevator starter, to use thereafter in order to correct any mistakes which the operator makes?

   A. Draw up a weekly list of the operator's mistakes and discuss the list with the operator at the end of each week
   B. Wait until the operator makes the same mistake twice before correcting it
   C. Discuss each of the operator's mistakes together with the other operators so that they will be helped also
   D. Explain the proper procedure to the operator as soon as possible after a mistake is made

18.____

19. Assume that a certain elevator starter is at work 8 hours a day, which includes 1 hour for lunch and two 15-minute relief periods. The rest of the workday the starter is performing his duties.
If the starter works 4 days, the TOTAL amount of time the starter will actually be performing his duties is _____ hours.

   A. 24   B. 26   C. 28   D. 32

19.____

20. Assume that a certain bank of 18 elevators operating at full capacity could move 3,240 passengers an hour from the main lobby.
The number of passengers that one of these elevators could move from the lobby every 15 minutes is, on the average,

   A. 12   B. 22   C. 45   D. 180

20.____

21. In a certain agency, the amount of absence due to injury or illness was an average of 6 hours a month for each employee.
If this agency had 335 employees, the TOTAL number of hours lost in a year due to injury or sickness was

   A. 4,020   B. 20,100   C. 24,120   D. 28,140

21.____

22. Assume that in a certain building the elevators must handle 16% of the building population during a peak traffic period.
If the building population is 2,825, the TOTAL number of people the elevators must handle during a peak traffic period is

   A. 396   B. 424   C. 436   D. 452

22.____

Questions 23-26

DIRECTIONS: Questions 23 through 26 are to be answered ONLY on the basis of the information given in the paragraph below.

The speed at which an elevator should run depends upon several considerations: the height of the building, the size of the building, the purpose for which the elevator will be used, and how the elevator will be used. Elevators with extremely high speeds are of little advantage unless an express run can be established to make use of it. On local runs, by the time an elevator accelerates and then decelerates for landing, there is little time to take advantage of speed. It should also be noted that the higher the elevator speed, the larger the machine, and hence the greater the cost. Therefore, the situation must be studied before each installation and the proper speed selected to avoid the purchase of unnecessary equipment.

23. According to the above paragraph, extremely high-speed elevators are of little advantage unless

    A. the building is small
    B. there are only two elevators in a large building
    C. they are used on express runs
    D. they accelerate and decelerate slowly on local runs

24. Which one of the following is NOT mentioned in the above paragraph as a consideration in selecting the speed at which an elevator should run?

    A. Height of the building   B. Age of the building
    C. Size of the building   D. Purpose of the elevator

25. Based on the paragraph, it would be MOST correct to say that a high-speed elevator _____ than a low-speed elevator.

    A. accelerates more slowly   B. uses less equipment
    C. breaks down more often   D. costs more

26. According to the above paragraph, one of the ways to avoid the purchase of unnecessary elevator equipment is to

    A. study the situation before each installation
    B. buy only low-speed elevators
    C. use smaller machines for high-speed elevators
    D. select low-speed elevators for express runs

Questions 27-30.

DIRECTIONS: Questions 27 through 30 are to be answered ONLY on the basis of the information given in the paragraph below.

Careful planning should always be given to the grouping of elevators in a building. When more than one elevator serves a building, the elevators should be located together as a single group or series of groups. Individual groups should be so arranged that the walking distance from the landing button to the furthermost elevator is kept at a minimum. The *alcove* arrangement, preferred for groups of five through eight elevators, has the advantage of preventing interference between people waiting for the elevators and people passing through the main corridor. It also holds *walking distance* to a minimum. The *straight line* arrangement is satisfactory for up to five cars. More than that will result in serious delays in service since the elevators must frequently wait while passengers walk from the extremities of the group.

27. According to the above paragraph, one way to prevent interference between people waiting for elevators and people using the main corridor is to

    A. use the *straight line* arrangement of elevators
    B. use the *alcove* arrangement of elevators

C. place the landing button next to the elevator farthest from the main corridor
D. eliminate the access from the main corridor to the elevator

28. According to the above paragraph, serious delays in elevator service may be caused by   28._____

    A. locating elevators together as a group or series of groups
    B. keeping *walking distance* to a minimum
    C. having six elevator cars in an *alcove* arrangement
    D. having seven elevator cars in a *straight line* arrangement

29. Based on the above paragraph, which of the following is the MOST accurate statement   29._____
    concerning the grouping of elevators in a building?

    A. The grouping of elevators always requires careful planning.
    B. Elevators should always be grouped in an *alcove* arrangement.
    C. Elevators should always be grouped in a *straight line* arrangement.
    D. A building should never contain more than eight elevators.

30. Based on the information given in the paragraph, which of the following is a preferred   30._____
    way of arranging twelve elevator cars in a building?

    A. All twelve cars in one *alcove*
    B. All twelve cars in a *straight line*
    C. Four cars in one *alcove* and eight cars in a *straight line*
    D. Six cars in each of two *alcoves*

KEY (CORRECT ANSWERS)

1. D	11. C	21. C
2. A	12. A	22. D
3. C	13. D	23. C
4. D	14. B	24. B
5. A	15. A	25. D
6. D	16. C	26. A
7. D	17. A	27. B
8. D	18. D	28. D
9. B	19. B	29. A
10. B	20. C	30. D

ELEVATOR MECHANICS

EXAMINATION SECTION
TEST 1

DIRECTIONS: Each question, or incomplete statement is followed by several suggested answers or completions. Select the one that *BEST* answers the question or completes the statement. *PRINT THE LETTER OF THE CORRECT ANSWER IN THE SPACE AT THE RIGHT.*

Questions 1-16.

DIRECTIONS: Questions 1 to 16 refer to the tools shown on page 2. (The numbers in the answer refer to the numbers beneath the tools. Tools are *NOT* drawn to scale.)

1. A 1" x 1" x 1/8" angle iron should be cut by using tool number   1.____
    A. A, 7   B. B, 12   C. 23   D. 42

2. To peen an iron rivet, you should use tool number   2.____
    A. 4   B. 7   C. 21   D. 43

3. The "star drill" is tool number   3.____
    A. 5.   B. 10   C. 20   D. 22

4. To make holes in sheet metal for sheet metal screws, you should use tool number   4.____
    A. 6   B. 10   C. 36   D. D, 46

5. To cut through a 3/8" diameter wire rope, you should use tool number   5.____
    A. 12   B. 23   C. 42   D. 54

6. To remove cutting burrs from the inside of a steel pipe, you should use tool number   6.____
    A. 5   B. 11   C. 14   D. 20

7. The depth of a bored hole may be measured *most accurately* with tool number   7.____
    A. 8   B. 16   C. 26   D. 41

8. If the marking on the blade of tool number 7 reads: "12-32," the 32 refers to the   8.____
    A. length   B. thickness
    C. weight   D. no. of teeth per inch

9. If tool number 6 bears the mark "5," it should be used to drill holes having a diameter of   9.____
    A. 5/32"   B. 5/16"   C. 5/8"   D. 5"

10. To determine *most quickly* the number of threads per inch on a bolt, you should use tool number   10.____
    A. 8   B. 16   C. 26   D. 50

77

11. Wood screws, located in positions where the headroom does not permit the use of an ordinary screwdriver, may be removed by using tool number

    A. 17 B. 28 C. 35 D. 46

12. To remove a broken-off piece of 1/2" diameter pipe from a fitting, you should use tool number

    A. 5 B. 11 C. 20 D. D, 36

13. The outside diameter of a bushing may be measured *most accurately* with tool number

    A. 8 B. 26 C. 33 D. 43

14. To rethread a stud hole in the casting of an elevator motor, you should use tool number

    A. 5 B. 20 C. 22 D. 36

TOOLS

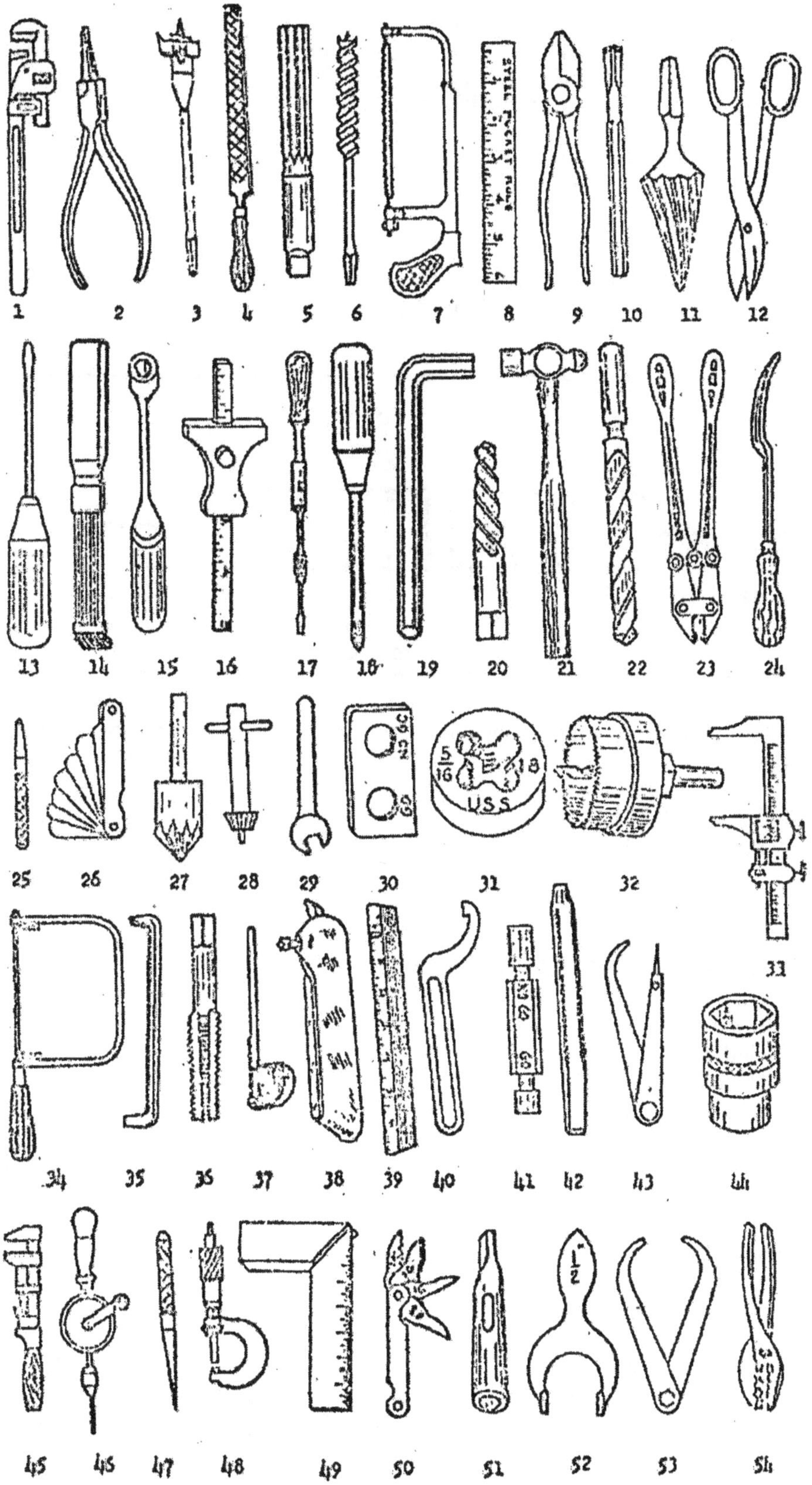
1 2 3 4 5 6 7 8 9 10 11 12
13 14 15 16 17 18 19 20 21 22 23 24
25 26 27 28 29 30 31 32
33
34 35 36 37 38 39 40 41 42 43 44
45 46 47 48 49 50 51 52 53 54

15. To enlarge *slightly* a bored hole in a steel plate, you should use tool number   15._____

    A. 5   B. 11   C. 20   D. D, 36

16. The term "16-oz." should be applied to tool number   16._____

    A. 1   B. 12   C. 21   D. 42

Questions 17-19.

DIRECTIONS: Questions 17 to 19 refer to the carbon resistor sketched below. Refer to this sketch when answering these questions.

17. Color coding is used on the resistor rather than having its rating printed on it MAINLY because the   17._____

    A. printing would fade in time
    B. color coding is simple to remember
    C. color coding prevents mix-ups
    D. resistor is too small for printing

18. Band number 3 on the resistor indicates the   18._____

    A. decimal multiplier
    B. third significant figure
    C. voltage rating
    D. percent tolerance

19. If band number 4 is missing from the resistor, it means that the resistor"s   19._____

    A. voltage is doubled
    B. voltage is zero
    C. tolerance is zero
    D. tolerance is 20 percent

20. The wire rope used for elevator hoisting consists of a number of wires laid into a strand, and a number of strands laid around a rope center. If the wires are laid left-handed into the strands, and the strands are laid right-handed around the rope center, the rope is called a   20._____

A. right-lay, regular-lay rope
B. left-lay, regular-lay rope
C. right-lay, Lang-lay rope
D. left-lay, Lang-lay rope

21. A *megger* should be used for the direct measurement of 21.____

    A. current   B. power   C. voltage   D. resistance

22. It is considered *bad* practice to use water to put out electrical fires *MAINLY* because the water may 22.____

    A. short-circuit the wires
    B. damage the insulation
    C. rust delicate equipment
    D. cause a serious electrical shock

23. Of the following, the method that should *NOT* be used to remove a length of hoist rope from its delivery reel is: 23.____

    A. Take off the rope from the top side while the reel is resting on its side
    B. Fix the free end and then roll the reel along the floor
    C. Mount the reel on a shaft and trunnions and then rotate the reel
    D. Mount the reel on a turntable and then rotate the turntable

24. The area of a circle, whose diameter is 24 inches, is, most nearly, 24.____

    A. 0.84 square foot
    B. 1.67 square feet
    C. 3.14 square feet
    D. 18.84 square feet

25. If an elevator mechanic opens the strands of a piece of manila rope and finds saw-dust material inside the rope, he should know that this means that the rope 25.____

    A. is relatively new
    B. has been damaged and should be discarded
    C. has dried out and must be re-oiled before use
    D. is to be used only for lights loads until the sawdust works itself out

26. Elevator mechanics are cautioned not to leave tools on scaffolding. The *MOST* important reason for this rule is to 26.____

    A. avoid a safety hazard
    B. prevent damage to the tools
    C. prevent theft of the tools
    D. prevent mix-ups in the mechanics' tools

Questions 27-40.

DIRECTIONS: Questions 27 to 40 are based on the sketch of a gearless elevator shown on page 6.

27. The *governor* is indicated by number 27.____
    A. 2   B. 7   C. 8   D. 16

28. The *motor generator* is indicated by number 28.____
    A. 1   B. 4   C. 7   D. 9

29. The *floor selector* is indicated by number 29.____
    A. 1   B. 2   C. 11   D. 16

30. The *hoistway limit switch* is indicated by number 30.____
    A. 8   B. 9   C. 10   D. 12

31. The *cable equalizer* is indicated by number 31.____
    A. 8   B. 9   C. 14   D. 26

32. The *brakes* are indicated by number 32.____
    A. 2   B. 5   C. 9   D. 22

33. The *buffers* are indicated by number 33.____
    A. 3   B. 9   C. 24   D. 25

34. The *compensating rope sheave* is indicated by number 34.____
    A. 8   B. 9   C. 25   D. 26

35. The *deflector sheave* is indicated by number 35.____
    A. 8   B. 9   C. 25   D. 26

36. The *door engines* are indicated by number 36.____
    A. 11   B. 12   C. 15   D. 16

37. The *guide shoes* are indicated by number 37.____
    A. 11   B. 12   C. 16   D. 20

38. The *music box* is indicated by number 38.____
    A. 3   B. 7   C. 11   D. 16

39. The *releasing carrier* is indicated by number 39.____
    A. 14   B. 16   C. 22   D. 27

40. The *rail grip shoes* are indicated by number 40.____
    A. 5   B. 17   C. 25   D. 26

7 (#1)

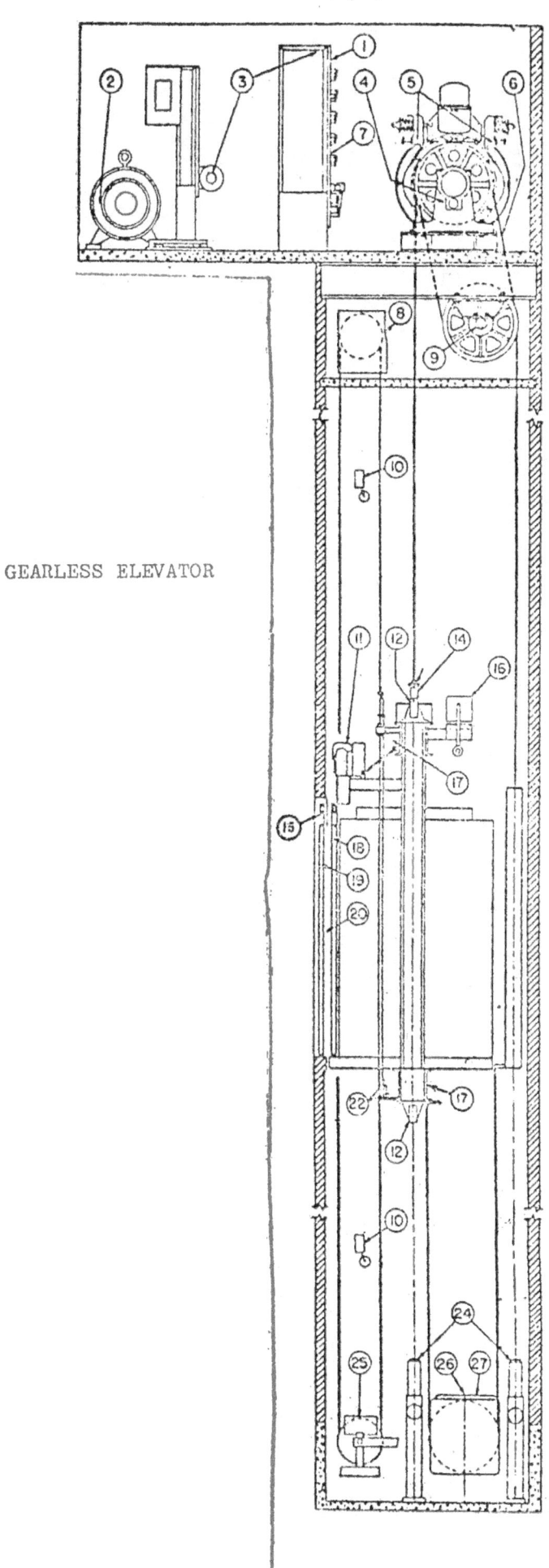

GEARLESS ELEVATOR

KEY (CORRECT ANSWER)

1. A	11. C	21. D	31. C
2. C	12. C	22. D	32. B
3. B	13. C	23. A	33. C
4. D	14. D	24. C	34. D
5. B	15. A	25. B	35. B
6. B	16. C	26. A	36. A
7. B	17. D	27. C	37. B
8. D	18. A	28. A	38. D
9. B	19. D	29. A	39. C
10. D	20. A	30. C	40. B

TEST 2

Questions 1-5.

DIRECTIONS: For Questions 1 to 5, the item referred to is shown to the right of the question.

1. The sketch shows a method of preventing a manila rope from unraveling. This is called
   A. splicing
   B. seizing
   C. mousing
   D. whipping

   1.____

2. The placing of a rope yarn on a hook to prevent the chain from being accidentally detached, as shown in the sketch, is called
   A. mousing
   B. whipping
   C. splicing
   D. seizing

   2.____

3. The knot shown is called a
   A. timber hitch
   B. clove hitch
   C. bowline
   D. becket

   3.____

4. The rigging device shown is a
   A. screw clamp
   B. shackle
   C. clevis
   D. thimble

   4.____

5. The wire-rope clip shown is a
   A. Crosby
   B. Loughlin
   C. Fist-grip
   D. C-clamp

   5.____

6. It is considered *good* practice to release the pressure from a hose containing compressed air before uncoupling the hose connection because this avoids

   A. damage to the air tool   B. damage to the air compressor
   C. wasting compressed air   D. possible personal injury

   6.____

7. Of the following electrical circuit components, the *one* which may give you an electrical shock even after the electrical power is turned off is a(n)

   A. charged capacitor   B. resistor
   C. interlock   D. relay

   7.____

Questions 8-14.

DIRECTIONS: For Questions 8 to 14, the item referred to is shown to the right of the question.

8. If the upper fuse is good and the lower fuse is burnt out, the test lamp that should be on is number
   A. 1
   B. 2
   C. 3
   D. 4

8.____

9. If the 1.5V battery has an internal resistance of 0.1 ohm and the 0.8V battery has an internal resistance of 0.3 ohm, then the current in the circuit is, most nearly,
   A. 0.2 amperes
   B. 1.8 amperes
   C. 4.2 amperes
   D. 17.5 amperes

9.____

10. If the 10-ohm resistor, marked X, burns out, the voltmeter reading will become, most nearly,
    A. 0
    B. 20
    C. 80
    D. 100

10.____

11. The total resistance in the circuit is, most nearly,
    A. 1.7 ohms
    B. 4.5 ohms
    C. 14 ohms
    D. 21 ohms

11.____

12. The power used by the heater is
    A. 120 watts
    B. 720 watts
    C. 2400 watts
    D. 4320 watts

12.____

13. If two amperes flow through the circuit, the terminal voltages is
    A. 2 volts
    B. 6 volts
    C. 12 volts
    D. 24 volts

13.____

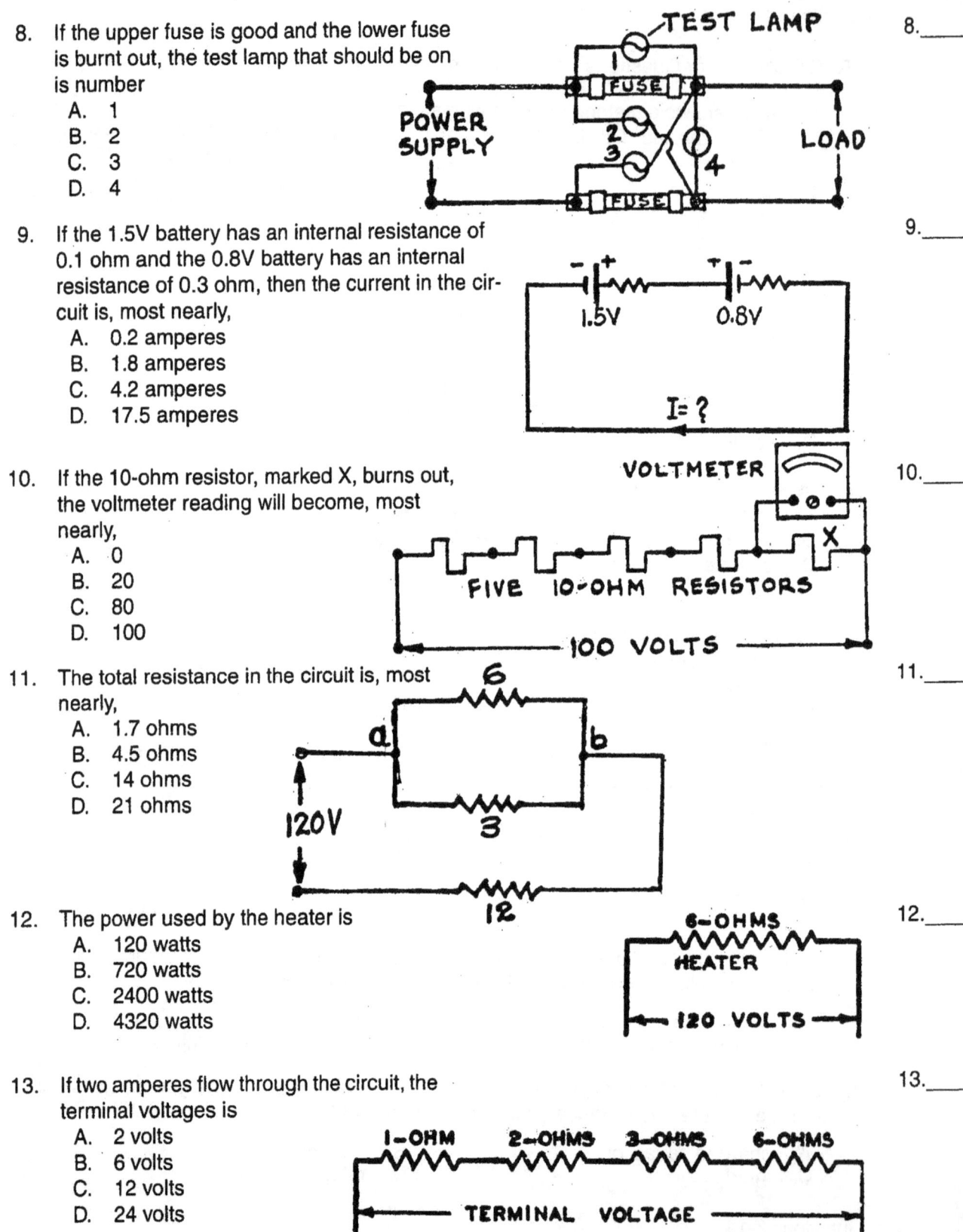

14. If the two voltmeters are identical, and the battery voltage is 120 volts, then the readings of the voltmeters should be
    A. 60 volts on each meter
    B. 120 volts on each meter
    C. 120 volts on meter #1, 240 volts on meter #2
    D. 120 volts on meter #1, zero volts on meter #2

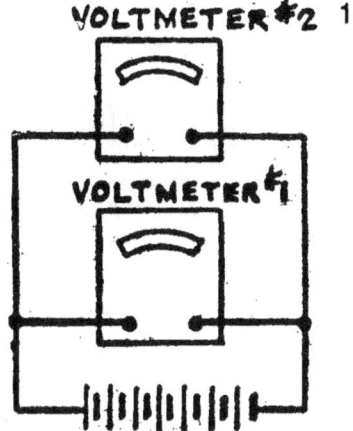

Questions 15-25.

DIRECTIONS: Questions 15 to 25 refer to the ELEVATOR WIRING DIAGRAM shown below. Refer to this diagram when answering these questions.

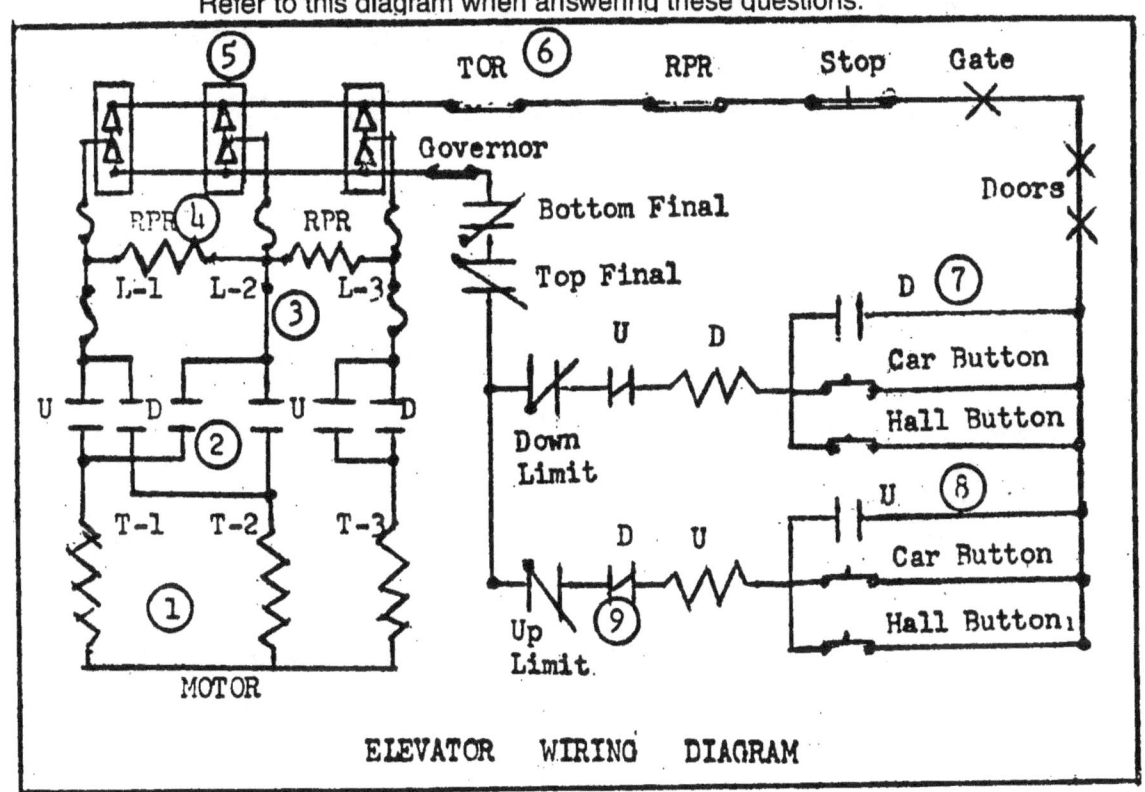

ELEVATOR WIRING DIAGRAM

15. The electrical symbol motor's  at ① indicates the motor's

    A. field windings
    B. electrical interlocks
    C. starting coil
    D. relay

16. The *MAIN* function of the wiring of L-l and L-2 through the U and D contactors at ② is to

    A. prevent overloading oiH;he motor
    B. permit reversing the motor
    C. prevent sharing the load between T-l, T-2
    D. permit different voltages to be applied

4 (#2)

17. The electrical symbols L-l, L-2 and L-3 at ③ indicate the

   A. power supply
   B. motor current
   C. circuit breakers
   D. line resistance

18. The MAIN function of the electrical component, labelled RPR at ④ is to

   A. prevent voltage changes in the circuit
   B. reduce the amount of current through the motor
   C. reverse the phases of the motor as the direction changes
   D. prevent elevator operation in case of reversa of the power supply phase

19. The MAIN function of the rectifiers at ⑤ is to

   A. reduce the voltage
   B. increase the current
   C. change A.C. to D.C.
   D. prevent current reversal

20. The MAIN function of the electrical component, labelled TOR at ⑥ is to

   A. prevent overspeeding
   B. cut in at terminal floor
   C. cut out at excessive torque
   D. prevent overheating

21. The arrangement of this circuit which prevents both the D contactor at ⑦ and the U contactor at ⑧ from being energized at the same time, is called a(n)

   A. interlock
   B. by-pass connection
   C. cross connection
   D. override

22. The pressing of the top-floor hall button while the car is descending will NOT prevent the elevator car from continuing downward because the

   A. down limit is closed
   B. D contact at ⑨ is opened
   C. down limit is opened
   D. D contact at ⑨ is closed

23. If the elevator car overspeeds, the safety device that should operate *first* is the

   A. Governor   B. Top final   C. Up limit   D. Stop

24. The MAIN function of the "Up Limit' and the "Down Limit" switch is to

   A. prevent the elevator car from hitting either pit or overhead

B. stop the elevator car nearly level with the landing
C. prevent the counterweight from hitting either at the top or bottom
D. keep the car speed within limits on the up and down trips

25. The "Bottom Final" and the "Top Final" switches are *usually* operated by

    A. the tiller rope B. the selector tape
    C. cams D. coils

26. It is considered *good* practice to lubricate elevator machinery

    A. during slack periods
    B. whenever it is needed
    C. at regularly scheduled times
    D. after a shut-down

27. Of the following, the *one* that should be used to dress a motor commutator is

    A. emery cloth B. sandpaper
    C. a flat file D. a mill file

28. A *tachometer* should be used for the direct measurement of

    A. torque B. power factor
    C. specific gravity D. r.p.m.

29. If 0.0375 is divided by 0.125, the result is

    A. 30.0 B. 3.0 C. 0.3 D. 0.03

30. It is considered *good* rigging practice to inspect chains more closely than wire rope prior to use MAINLY because chains

    A. twist more easily B. stretch more
    C. rust more readily D. have less reserve strength

31. A *hydrometer* should be used for the *direct* measurement of

    A. A torque B. power factor
    C. r.p.m. D. specific gravity

32. Of the following, elevator hoisting cables should be lubricated with

    A. a heavy grease B. medium-heavy oil
    C. graphite D. tar

33. If you were directed to check the "backlash" on an elevator hoisting motor, you should check the

    A. gears B. bearings C. contactors D. brakes

34. The MAIN function of a "pole shader" on a coil is to

    A. prevent heating B. prevent hum
    C. reduce resistance D. reduce flux

Questions 35-40.

DIRECTIONS: Questions 35 to 40 refer to the elevator CALL BUTTON CIRCUIT shown below. Refer to this circuit when answering these questions.

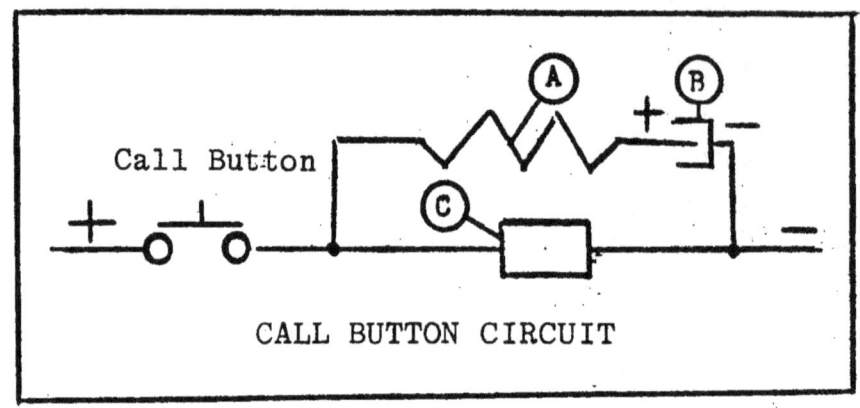

CALL BUTTON CIRCUIT

35. The electrical component shown at A is a

   A. resistor   B. coil   C. condenser   D. contactor

36. The electrical component shown at B is a

   A. resistor   B. coil   C. condenser   D. contactor

37. The electrical component shown at C is a

   A. resistor   B. coil   C. condenser   D. contactor

38. The MAIN purpose of component A is to

   A. short circuit B
   C. reduce voltage to C
   B. limit current to B
   D. increase current to C

39. The MAIN purpose of component B is to

   A. time the circuit
   B. increase the voltage
   C. decrease button resistance
   D. interrupt the circuit

40. The MAIN purpose of component C is to

   A. reduce the current
   B. increase the voltage
   C. open and close contactors
   D. reverse current polarity

KEY (CORRECT ANSWERS)

1. D	11. C	21. A	31. D
2. A	12. C	22. B	32. B
3. C	13. D	23. A	33. A
4. B	14. B	24. B	34. A
5. A	15. A	25. C	35. A
6. D	16. B	26. C	36. C
7. A	17. A	27. B	37. B
8. C	18. D	28. D	38. B
9. B	19. C	29. C	39. A
10. D	20. D	30. D	40. C

EXAMINATION SECTION
TEST 1

DIRECTIONS: Each question or incomplete statement is followed by several suggested answers or completions. Select the one that BEST answers the question or completes the statement. *PRINT THE LETTER OF THE CORRECT ANSWER IN THE SPACE AT THE RIGHT.*

1. Elevator machinery and related equipment is BEST lubricated 1.____

    A. whenever it is required
    B. after a shut-down
    C. during slack work periods
    D. at scheduled times

2. The direction of rotation of a D.C. shunt motor can be *reversed* by reversing 2.____

    A. the line connections
    B. both the field and the armature connections
    C. either the field or the armature connections
    D. the residual field

3. The bearings of geared type hoist motors are MOST usually of the _____ type. 3.____

    A. sleeve   B. ball bearing
    C. ball and roller   D. tapered roller

4. Installation of a Type A (instantaneous) car safety is limited to cars operating at speeds, in FPM, between _____ and _____. 4.____

    A. 0; 120   B. 130; 150   C. 175; 300   D. 150; 500

5. Of the following statements concerning the use of rubber-tired roller guides, the one which is MOST NEARLY correct is that their use would 5.____

    A. increase electric power usage
    B. help prevent hoistway fires
    C. increase maintenance costs
    D. require lubrication of the rails

6. Of the following grades of carbon steel wire rope, the one which contains the LEAST percentage of carbon is 6.____

    A. traction   B. improved plow
    C. plow   D. iron

7. In checking the neutral position of the carbon brushes in a variable voltage elevator hoist motor, a voltohmmeter is to be used as a test meter.
Of the following meter scales, the CORRECT one to use would be the _____ scale. 7.____

    A. 50-microamp   B. 10-milliamp
    C. 10-amp   D. 15-amp

8. The rating of a standard cartridge fuse having a navy blue paper label is 8.____

A. 250 volts, 30 amperes capacity
B. 250 volts, 15 amperes or less capacity
C. 250 volts, over 15 amperes capacity
D. 120 volts, 15 amperes capacity

9. In ordering a standard cartridge fuse, it is MOST necessary to specify the

   A. minimum length of ferrule and outside diameter of tube
   B. power factor of the connected load
   C. voltage of the circuit and the current capacity
   D. type of construction and the tolerance

10. Of the following substances, the BEST one to use to make it easier to pull wire conductors through electric conduit is

    A. powdered soapstone   B. petroleum jelly
    C. light oil   D. powdered graphite

11. A *Brinell test* is used to determine the

    A. hardness of metals
    B. strength of carbon brushes
    C. accuracy of tachometers
    D. number of broken wires in a rope

12. Of the following materials, the one which is NOT commonly used to line elevator brake shoes is

    A. asbestos   B. leather   C. wood   D. teflon

13. In a worm and gear elevator machine, metallic contact between the worm and the gear teeth is LEAST likely to occur when the oil level in the gear case is

    A. touching the bottom of the worm
    B. level with the center line of the worm-shaft
    C. level with the gear case drain plug
    D. between the bottom of the gear case and the bottom of the worm

14. The diameter of the hole of a bronze sleeve bearing is
    $2.402"{}^{+.006"}_{-.000"}$ and the diameter of the shaft for this bearing
    is $2.401"{}^{+.000"}_{-.003"}$.
    The limits of the clearance for the shaft in the bearing are MOST NEARLY _____" max; _____" min.

    A. .010; .001   B. .001; .001
    C. .007; .004   D. .006; .003

15. Of the following, the PRIMARY purpose of assigning mechanics to perform periodic inspection and testing of elevator equipment is to

    A. keep the mechanics active during slack periods
    B. provide on-the-job training for the less experienced mechanics

C. evaluate the mechanics' knowledge of the equipment
D. uncover potential equipment faults before they develop into major breakdowns

16. Of the following lubricants, the BEST one to use to lubricate elevator traction machine wire ropes is a

    A. heavy body oil mixed with graphite
    B. heavy body oil mixed with sulphur
    C. thin to medium heavy petroleum oil mixed with animal or vegetable oil
    D. very thin opaque oil mixed with a small quantity of pine tar

17. A megger tester is an instrument that is used to

    A. measure electrical insulation resistance
    B. determine the resistance of a bare copper conductor
    C. measure the rotative speed of a shaft
    D. determine the value of capacitors

18. When a mechanic is trained for a particular job, it is important that the mechanic be instructed properly. Listed below are four basic steps, in scrambled order, in training a worker:
    I. Demonstrate the actual operation to the mechanic
    II. Periodically check on the mechanic's performance
    III. Have the mechanic practice the job himself
    IV. Interest the mechanic in the job
    The CORRECT order in which these steps should be taken is

    A. II, I, III, IV
    B. III, I, IV, II
    C. II, IV, I, III
    D. IV, I, III, II

19. A suggestion is made that a machine be installed in the shop to help the mechanics on the job. You feel that the suggestion is a good one but realize that you cannot get the machine immediately, but that you may be able to obtain one at a later date.
    Of the following, the MOST effective way to handle the situation is to tell the mechanic that

    A. it is a good idea and to remind you of the suggestion at some other time
    B. you will look into the possibility and let him know if and when one can be installed
    C. the suggestion cannot be considered at the present time
    D. the shop does not require the machine and that none will be installed

20. One of the mechanics has just touched a bare electric wire carrying power and cannot let go.
    The one of the following actions that should be taken FIRST to assist the injured man is to

    A. use a dry rope or dry stick to remove the victim from the electrical source
    B. treat the mechanic for burns
    C. start artificial respiration or mouth-to-mouth breathing
    D. cut off the power, but only if it takes 5 minutes or less to find the switch

21. When lifting heavy objects without mechanical equipment, it is SAFEST to

    A. keep your back bent and knees straight

B. keep your feet as far from the object as possible
C. lift the object as fast as possible
D. use both arm and leg muscle

22. Of the following, the CHIEF cause of accidents on the job is 22.___

    A. faulty construction of elevator shafts
    B. mechanical failure of work equipment
    C. unsafe acts on the part of the workers
    D. improper work schedules

23. Assume that the men are being trained in the safe use of the ladder. 23.___
    According to accepted safety practice, if you place a 12-foot ladder against a wall, the distance between the foot of the ladder and the wall should be MOST NEARLY _____ foot(feet).

    A. 1   B. 3   C. 6   D. 9

24. Of the following types of portable fire extinguishers, the one which is the MOST suitable 24.___
    type for putting out *live* electrical wiring fires is a Class _____ extinguisher.

    A. A   B. B   C. C   D. D

25. Assume that you have been asked by the superintendent of a housing project to partici- 25.___
    pate in a tenants' meeting regarding elevator vandalism.
    Of the following types of meetings, the one that will MOST likely have the highest tenant participation is the _____ type meeting.

    A. speaker-and-panel   B. formal conference
    C. open-discussion   D. speaker-only

KEY (CORRECT ANSWERS)

1. D		11. A
2. C		12. D
3. A		13. B
4. A		14. A
5. B		15. D
6. D		16. C
7. B		17. A
8. B		18. D
9. C		19. B
10. A		20. A

21. D
22. C
23. B
24. C
25. C

TEST 2

DIRECTIONS: Each question or incomplete statement is followed by several suggested answers or completions. Select the one that BEST answers the question or completes the statement. *PRINT THE LETTER OF THE CORRECT ANSWER IN THE SPACE AT THE RIGHT.*

1. The traveling crosshead or nut of a selector machine is driven vertically up and down by a

    A. flexible connection between the driving sheave and the car
    B. magnetically operated switch located on each landing
    C. steel tape attached to the car and wound on the sheaves at the top of the hoistway
    D. series of cold-cathode tubes electrically connected to a metal strip installed on the leading edge of the car door

    1._____

2. Assume that 8 mechanics have been assigned to do a job that must be finished in 5 days. At the end of 3 days, the men have completed only half the job.
   In order to complete the job on time in the remaining 2 days, the MINIMUM number of extra men that should be assigned is

    A. 2   B. 3   C. 4   D. 6

    2._____

3. Assume that the air gap between the stator and the bottom of the rotor of an A.C. motor is 0.01" less than a previously recorded clearance.
   This lessening of the air gap would MOST likely indicate that the

    A. spring tension holding the carbon brushes is excessive
    B. bearings of the motor are wearing
    C. stator laminations need to be replaced
    D. terminal voltage to the motor is too high

    3._____

4. Of the following types of wire-rope construction, the one recommended for double-wrap traction machines with sheaves under 30 inches in diameter is the

    A. 6 x 19 Warrington   B. 6 x 27 Regular
    C. 8 x 19 Seale   D. 8 x 25 Filler

    4._____

5. Upon inspecting an electrical contact in an elevator control circuit, you notice that the contact has a coating that is a dark bluish-black color.
   For this particular contact, it would be BEST to

    A. dress the contact by filing lightly with a double-cut smooth file
    B. mechanically open and close the contact periodically to break up the coating
    C. wipe the contact with a soft cloth
    D. leave the coating on the contact since it is a good conductor

    5._____

6. In a worm-gear elevator machine, the gear is GENERALLY machined from castings made of

    A. bronze   B. alloy steel   C. cast iron   D. copper

    6._____

7. An elevator supply manufacturer quotes a list price of $625 less 10 and 5 percent for ten contactors.
   The actual cost for these ten contactors is MOST NEARLY

    7._____

97

A. $562   B. $554   C. $534   D. $522

8. Assume that a rectifier has been disconnected from a circuit. Of the following meters, the one which should be used in checking the serviceability of this rectifier is a(n)

   A. ohmmeter
   B. AC voltmeter
   C. ammeter
   D. DC voltmeter

9. The length of a wire rope lay is APPROXIMATELY equal to _____ times the diameter of the rope.

   A. $3\frac{1}{2}$ B. $4\frac{1}{2}$ C. $5\frac{1}{2}$ D. $6\frac{1}{2}$

10. A generator that develops the same voltage at no load and at maximum load, but with a peak voltage in between, is called a(n) _____ compounded generator.

    A. differential   B. under   C. over   D. flat

Questions 11-17.

DIRECTIONS: Questions 11 to 17 are to be answered in accordance with the diagram shown below.

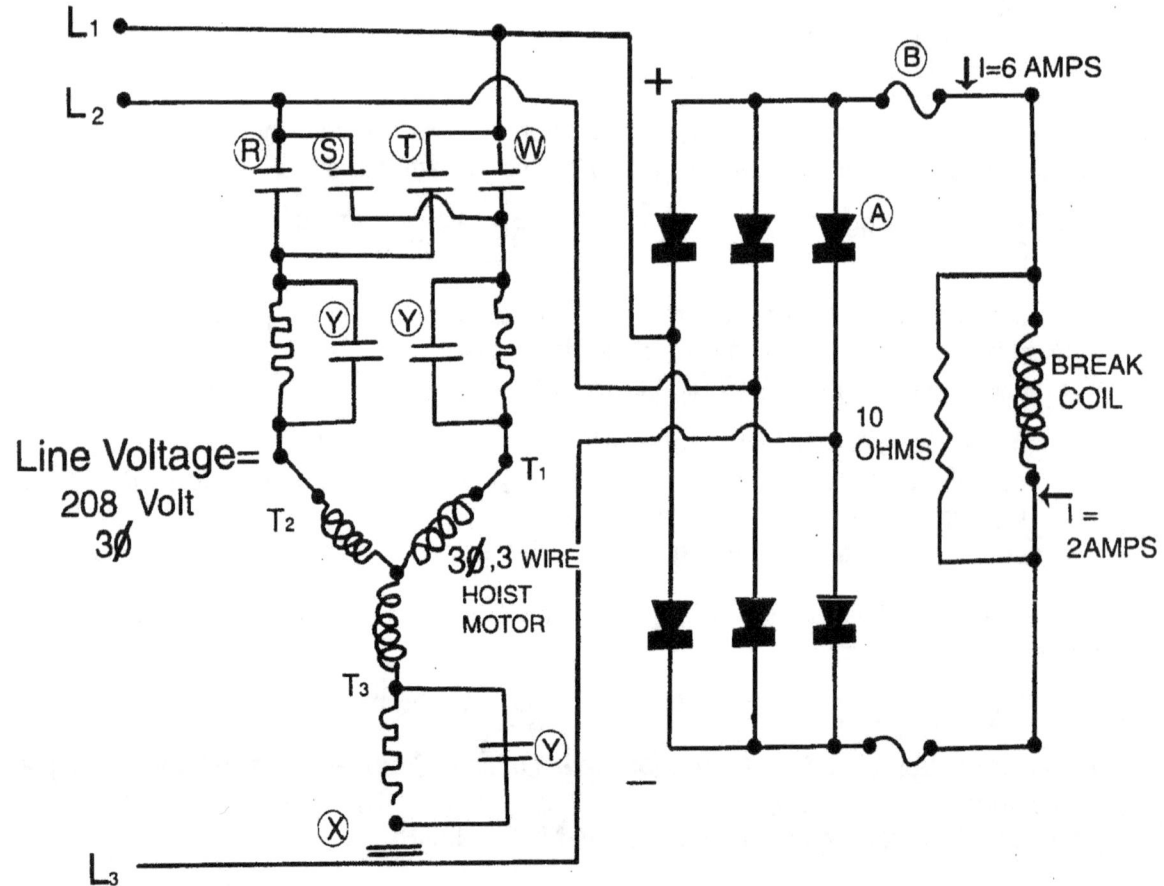

11. Each of the three contacts labeled Y in the above diagram are across a resistor. With respect to the operation of the hoist motor, these contacts should be

    A. closed when starting, open when running
    B. open when starting, closed when running
    C. closed when stopping, open when running
    D. open when stopping, open when running

12. Symbols such as the one labeled A in the above diagram USUALLY represent

    A. limit switches   B. detectors
    C. interlocks   D. rectifiers

13. The voltage across each of the hoist motor's three stator windings in the above diagram, when connected directly across the line, is MOST NEARLY _____ volts.

    A. 104   B. 120   C. 208   D. 416

14. Assume that the 3-phase hoist motor runs clockwise when contactors R, W, and X are closed, and contacts S and T are open.
    Of the following conditions, the one which will cause the motor to rotate in the OPPOSITE direction is

    A. open R, W, and X, close S and T
    B. open R, S, and T, close W and X
    C. close S, T, and X, open R and W
    D. close R, T, and W, open S and X

15. In the above diagram, the combined resistance of the brake coil and the 10-ohm resistor is MOST NEARLY _____ ohms.

    A. 5   B. 6 2/3   C. 10   D. 16 2/3

16. In the above diagram, the resistance of the brake coil is MOST NEARLY _____ ohms.

    A. zero   B. 10   C. 20   D. 30

17. In the above diagram, if the current through the fuse B is 6 amps, as shown, and the current through the brake coil is 2 amps, the voltage across the brake coil will be MOST NEARLY _____ volts.

    A. 2   B. 4
    C. 10   D. none of the above

18. Assume that you are meeting with a tenant group to explain a new, improved system of elevator maintenance for their building.
    Of the following, the LEAST effective method of maintaining the interest of this group is to

    A. concentrate only on the disadvantages of old elevator maintenance services
    B. show them how the new maintenance service will benefit them
    C. let them know what areas of the new maintenance plan you will discuss
    D. use visual aids to explain the new elevator maintenance service

19. Assume that, at a meeting with a tenant group, you are leading an open discussion on finding ways to reduce vandalism to the project's elevators.
Of the following practices, the BEST one for you to follow in leading the discussion is to

   A. make your suggestions, then give the group a chance to make theirs
   B. comment on and evaluate the contributions of members of the group to the discussion
   C. tell the group how they should operate as a discussion group
   D. encourage members of the group to speak out on the matter

20. You are asked to speak on ways to combat vandalism at a community housing project meeting.
Of the following, the BEST way to assure that the audience remembers the main points of your speech is to

   A. ask someone in the audience to read a written summary of the speech before you start speaking
   B. summarize the major points of your discussion at the end of your speech
   C. take a break during your speech and summarize the entire speech so far
   D. repeat what you have said every few paragraphs

21. The one of the following that is the MOST important characteristic of communication is that it

   A. involves just the sending of messages from one person to another
   B. transmits both information and understanding from one person to another
   C. helps the men adjust to work rules and procedures
   D. is concerned with the writing of clear, easy-to-read statements

22. The following are four important steps, in scrambled order, in the planning of a work project:
   I. Schedule the work
   II. Gather the facts
   III. Define the problem
   IV. Evaluate the facts

   The CORRECT order in which these steps should be taken to do the work project properly is

   A. III, II, IV, I   B. IV, III, II, I
   C. I, III, II, IV   D. II, III, IV, I

23. The one of the following that is commonly considered to be the MOST serious result of a mechanic's being frequently absent is that

   A. the supervisor may become unconcerned about the employee
   B. the employee in question may worry about his being late
   C. work schedules may be disrupted
   D. re-training of the employee will be necessary

24. Of the following, the BEST way to reduce the number of rumors related to work matters among mechanics is for supervisors to

    A. have the mechanics publish a bulletin describing all rumors presently circulating so that everything is *out in the open*
    B. supply accurate information to the mechanics as soon as possible on matters that are important to them
    C. constantly change their official interpretations of work matters so that the mechanics will not have any basis for rumors
    D. informally confide in their mechanics more often

25. According to the standard procedure manual, the symbol *N*, when used to record overtime work in the elevator log book, indicates

    A. night work differential
    B. nuisance
    C. necessary approval was granted
    D. no materials used

KEY (CORRECT ANSWERS)

1. C	11. B
2. C	12. D
3. B	13. B
4. C	14. C
5. D	15. B
6. A	16. C
7. C	17. D
8. A	18. A
9. D	19. D
10. D	20. B

21. B
22. A
23. C
24. B
25. B

EXAMINATION SECTION
TEST 1

DIRECTIONS: This test consists of 8 essay questions, all of which are of equal weight. Answer all of the questions fully and completely. The allotted time of 4 hours for completion of this test allows an AVERAGE of 30 minutes for each question.

In writing your answers, bear in mind that your rating will depend on the thoroughness of your analysis, the proper weighing of the factors involved, the logic and justification of your decisions or conclusions and the quality of the written presentation. No credit will be given for repetition and useless detail. If a specific number of responses is required in a question, give only the required number of responses called for. If you give more than the specific number of responses, only the required number will be rated in the order in which they appear on the answer sheet. For example, if you are required to list five reasons but your answer contains more than five reasons, only the first five reasons will be rated.

In answering each question, you are to assume that you are an Assistant Supervisor (Elevators and Escalators) in the New York City Transit Authority.

1. When inspecting an elevator hoist rope, what factors should be considered in determining whether it should be replaced?

2. You question a foreman about the operational failure of an elevator. The foreman claims that the cause was poor maintenance by the maintainers assigned to that elevator. Discuss the complete course of action that you should take in this situation.

3. Assume that you have been assigned to review the existing maintenance procedures of the Elevator and Escalator Subdivision for the purpose of cutting maintenance costs. However, this is to be achieved without lowering either performance or safety standards. Describe those conditions which would make it advisable to revise existing maintenance procedures.

4. Assume that extensive reconditioning work on an escalator is scheduled at a busy station and will take about three months. Describe the planning which will be necessary to do this job. In your description, indicate what problems should be anticipated and explain how these problems should be handled.

5. Assume that one of your experienced foremen has been doing unsatisfactory work for the last few weeks. Although you have criticized his poor work on several occasions, his performance has not improved. You decide to call this foreman to your office to discuss his work. How should you conduct this discussion and what points should you cover if your purpose is to improve this foreman's work performance?

6. Whenever the regular electrical power to a Transit Authority elevator fails, the elevator can be operated by emergency power. What is the source of the emergency power; how is the transfer to emergency power made in both operator and non-operator elevators; what elevator equipment is involved in the transfer; how are the regular electrical circuits changed in the transfer; and how long can emergency power be provided?

7. Records and reports are effective tools for the efficient management of the work of the Elevator and Escalator Subdivision. If properly used, these records and reports will alert an Assistant Supervisor to potential sources of trouble, and will pinpoint any deficiencies in his maintenance program. Select five of the reports available to an Assistant Supervisor and for each one explain how it should be helpful to him in effectively supervising his maintenance program.

8. Describe the measures that you should take to minimize the number of accidents in the Elevator and Escalator Subdivision.

SAFETY
EXAMINATION SECTION
TEST 1

DIRECTIONS: Each question or incomplete statement is followed by several suggested answers or completions. Select the one that BEST answers the question or completes the statement. *PRINT THE LETTER OF THE CORRECT ANSWER IN THE SPACE AT THE RIGHT.*

1. Which one of the following is an INCORRECT safety guideline?   1.____

    A. All working conditions and equipment should be considered carefully before beginning an operation.
    B. Aisles should be lighted properly.
    C. Personnel should be provided with protective clothing essential to safe performance of a task.
    D. In manual lifting, the worker must keep his knees straight and lift with the arm muscles.

2. Of the following, the supply item with the GREATEST susceptibility to spontaneous heating is   2.____

    A. alcohol, ethyl   B. kerosene
    C. candles   D. turpentine

Questions 3-7.

DIRECTIONS: Questions 3 through 7 are descriptions of accidents that occurred in a warehouse. For each accident, choose the letter in front of the safety measure that is MOST likely to prevent a repetition of the accident indicated.

SAFETY MEASURE

    A. Posting warning signs
    B. Redesign of layout or facilities
    C. Repairing, improving or replacing supplies, tools or equipment
    D. Training the staff in safe practices

3. After a new all-glass door was installed at the entrance to the warehouse, one of the employees banged his head into the door causing a large lump on his forehead when he failed to realize that the door was closed.   3.____

4. While tieing up a package with manila rope, an employee got several small rope splinters in his right hand and he had to have medical treatment to remove the splinters.   4.____

5. An employee discovered a small fire in a wastepaper basket but was unable to prevent it from spreading because all the nearby fire extinguishers were inaccessible due to skids of material being stacked in front of the extinguishers.   5.____

6. When a laborer attempted to drop the tailgate of a delivery truck while the truck was being backed into the loading dock, he had his fingers crushed when the truck continued to move while he was working on lowering the tailgate.   6.____

105

7. An employee carrying a carton with both hands tripped over a broom which had been left lying in an aisle by another employee after the latter had swept the aisle.   7.___

8. Safety experts agree that accidents can probably BEST be prevented by   8.___

   A. developing safety consciousness among employees
   B. developing a program which publicizes major accidents
   C. penalizing employees the first time they do not follow safety procedures
   D. giving recognition to employees with accident-free records

9. The accident records of many agencies indicate that most on-the-job injuries are caused by the unsafe acts of their employees.
Which one of the following statements pinpoints the MOST probable cause of this safety problem?   9.___

   A. Responsibility for preventing on-the-job accidents has not been delegated.
   B. Lack of proper supervision has permitted these unsafe actions to continue.
   C. No consideration has been given to eliminating environmental job hazards.
   D. Penalties for causing on-the-job accidents are not sufficiently severe.

10. Which of the following methods is LEAST essential to the success of an accident prevention program?   10.___

    A. Determining corrective measures by analyzing the causes of accidents and making recommendations to eliminate them
    B. Educating employees as to the importance of safe working conditions and methods
    C. Determining accident causes by seeking out the conditions from which each accident has developed
    D. Holding each supervisor responsible for accidents occurring during the on-the-job performance of his immediate subordinates

11. The effectiveness of a public relations program in a public agency is BEST indicated by the   11.___

    A. amount of mass media publicity favorable to the policies of the agency
    B. morale of those employees who directly serve the patrons of the agency
    C. public's understanding and support of the agency's program and policies
    D. number of complaints received by the agency from patrons using its facilities

12. Buttered bread and coffee dropped on an office floor in a terminal are   12.___

    A. minor hazards which should cause no serious injury
    B. unattractive, but not dangerous
    C. the most dangerous types of office hazards
    D. hazards which should be corrected immediately

13. A laborer was sent upstairs to get a 20-pound sack of rock salt. While going downstairs and reading the printing on the sack, he fell, and the sack of rock salt fell and broke his toe.
Which of the following is MOST likely to have been the MOST important cause of the accident?
The   13.___

A. stairs were beginning to become worn
B. laborer was carrying too heavy a sack of rock salt
C. rock salt was in a place that was too inaccessible
D. laborer was not careful about the way he went down the stairs

14. A COMMONLY recommended safe distance between the foot of an extension ladder and the wall against which it is placed is

    A. 3 feet for ladders less than 18 feet in height
    B. between 3 feet and 6 feet for ladders less than 18 feet in length
    C. 1/8 the length of the extended ladder
    D. 1/4 the length of the extended ladder

15. The BEST type of fire extinguisher for electrical fires is the _____ extinguisher.

    A. dry chemical   B. foam
    C. carbon monoxide   D. baking soda-acid

16. A Class A extinguisher should be used for fires in

    A. potassium, magnesium, zinc, sodium
    B. electrical wiring
    C. oil, gasoline
    D. wood, paper, and textiles

17. The one of the following which is NOT a safe practice when lifting heavy objects is:

    A. Keep the back as nearly upright as possible
    B. If the object feels too heavy, keep lifting until you get help
    C. Spread the feet apart
    D. Use the arm and leg muscles

18. In a shop, it would be MOST necessary to provide a fitted cover on the metal container for

    A. old paint brushes   B. oily rags and waste
    C. sand   D. broken glass

19. Safety shoes usually have the unique feature of

    A. extra hard heels and soles to prevent nails from piercing the shoes
    B. special leather to prevent the piercing of the shoes by falling objects
    C. a metal guard over the toes which is built into the shoes
    D. a non-slip tread on the heels and soles

20. Of the following, the MOST important factor contributing to a helper's safety on the job is for him to

    A. work slowly   B. wear gloves
    C. be alert   D. know his job well

21. If it is necessary for you to lift one end of a piece of heavy equipment with a crowbar in order to allow a maintainer to work underneath it, the BEST of the following procedures to follow is to

    A. support the handle of the bar on a box
    B. insert temporary blocks to support the piece
    C. call the supervisor to help you
    D. wear heavy gloves

22. Of the following, the MOST important reason for not letting oily rags accumulate in an open storage bin is that they

    A. may start a fire by spontaneous combustion
    B. will drip oil onto other items in the bin
    C. may cause a foul odor
    D. will make the area messy

23. Of the following, the BEST method to employ in putting out a gasoline fire is to

    A. use a bucket of water
    B. smother it with rags
    C. use a carbon dioxide extinguisher
    D. use a carbon tetrachloride extinguisher

24. When opening an emergency exit door set in the sidewalk, the door should be raised slowly to avoid

    A. a sudden rush of air from the street
    B. making unnecessary noise
    C. damage to the sidewalk
    D. injuring pedestrians

25. The BEST reason to turn off lights when cleaning lampshades on electrical fixtures is to

    A. conserve energy
    B. avoid electrical shock
    C. prevent breakage of lightbulbs
    D. prevent unnecessary eye strain

KEY (CORRECT ANSWERS)

1. D
2. D
3. A
4. D
5. B

6. D
7. D
8. A
9. B
10. D

11. C
12. D
13. D
14. D
15. A

16. D
17. B
18. B
19. C
20. C

21. B
22. A
23. C
24. D
25. B

TEST 2

DIRECTIONS: Each question or incomplete statement is followed by several suggested answers or completions. Select the one that BEST answers the question or completes the statement. *PRINT THE LETTER OF THE CORRECT ANSWER IN THE SPACE AT THE RIGHT.*

1. The MOST important reason for roping off a work area in a terminal is to
    A. protect the public
    B. protect the repair crew
    C. prevent distraction of the crew by the public
    D. prevent delays to the public

2. Shoes which have a sponge rubber sole should NOT be worn around a work area because such a sole
    A. will wear quickly
    B. is not waterproof
    C. does not keep the feet warm
    D. is easily punctured by steel objects

3. When repair work is being done on an elevated structure, canvas spreads are suspended under the working area MAINLY to
    A. reduce noise
    B. discourage crowds
    C. protect the structure
    D. protect pedestrians

4. It is poor practice to hold a piece of wood in the hands or lap when tightening a screw in the wood.
   This is for the reason that
    A. sufficient leverage cannot be obtained
    B. the screwdriver may bend
    C. the wood will probably split
    D. personal injury is likely to result

5. Steel helmets give workers the MOST protection from
    A. falling objects
    B. eye injuries
    C. fire
    D. electric shock

6. It is POOR practice to wear goggles
    A. when chipping stone
    B. when using a grinder
    C. while climbing or descending ladders
    D. when handling molten metal

7. When using a brace and bit to bore a hole completely through a partition, it is MOST important to

A. lean heavily on the brace and bit
B. maintain a steady turning speed all through the job
C. have the body in a position that will not be easily thrown off balance
D. reverse the direction of the bit at frequent intervals

8. Gloves should be used when handling

A. lanterns
B. wooden rules
C. heavy ropes
D. all small tools

Questions 9-16.

DIRECTIONS: Questions 9 through 16, inclusive, are based on the ladder safety rules given below. Read these rules fully before answering these items.

LADDER SAFETY RULES

When a ladder is placed on a slightly uneven supporting surface, use a flat piece of board or small wedge to even up the ladder feet. To secure the proper angle for resting a ladder, it should be placed so that the distance from the base of the ladder to the supporting wall is 1/4 the length of the ladder. To avoid overloading a ladder, only one person should work on a ladder at a time. Do not place a ladder in front of a door. When the top rung of a ladder rests against a pole, the ladder should be lashed securely. Clear loose stones or debris from the ground around the base of a ladder before climbing. While on a ladder, do not attempt to lean so that any part of the body, except arms or hands, extends more than 12 inches beyond the side rail. Always face the ladder when ascending or descending. When carrying ladders through buildings, watch for ceiling globes and lighting fixtures. Avoid the use of rolling ladders as scaffold supports.

9. A small wedge is used to

A. even up the feet of a ladder resting on an uneven surface
B. lock the wheels of a roller ladder
C. secure the proper resting angle for a ladder
D. secure a ladder against a pole

10. An 8 foot ladder resting against a wall should be so inclined that the distance between the base of the ladder and the wall is _____ feet.

A. 2   B. 5   C. 7   D. 9

11. A ladder should be lashed securely when

A. it is placed in front of a door
B. loose stones are on the ground near the base of the ladder
C. the top rung rests against a pole
D. two people are working from the same ladder

12. Rolling ladders

A. should be used for scaffold supports
B. should not be used for scaffold supports
C. are useful on uneven ground
D. should be used against a pole

13. When carrying a ladder through a building, it is necessary to

    A. have two men to carry it
    B. carry the ladder vertically
    C. watch for ceiling globes
    D. face the ladder while carrying it

14. It is POOR practice to

    A. lash a ladder securely at any time
    B. clear debris from the base of a ladder before climbing
    C. even up the feet of a ladder resting on slightly uneven ground
    D. place a ladder in front of a door

15. A person on a ladder should NOT extend his head beyond the side rail by more than _____ inches.

    A. 12   B. 9   C. 7   D. 5

16. The MOST important reason for permitting only one person to work on a ladder at a time is that

    A. both could not face the ladder at one time
    B. the ladder will be overloaded
    C. time would be lost going up and down the ladder
    D. they would obstruct each other

17. Many portable electric power tools, such as electric drills, have a third conductor in the power lead which is used to connect the case of the tool to a grounded part of the electric outlet.
    The reason for this extra conductor is to

    A. have a spare wire in case one power wire should break
    B. strengthen the power lead so it cannot easily be damaged
    C. prevent the user of the tool from being shocked
    D. enable the tool to be used for long periods of time without overheating

18. Protective goggles should NOT be worn when

    A. standing on a ladder drilling a steel beam
    B. descending a ladder after completing a job
    C. chipping concrete near a third rail
    D. sharpening a cold chisel on a grinding stone

19. When the foot of an extension ladder, placed against a high wall, rests on a sidewalk or another such similar surface, it is advisable to tie a rope between the bottom rung of the ladder and a point on the wall opposite this rung.
    This is done to prevent

    A. people from walking under the ladder
    B. another worker from removing the ladder
    C. the ladder from vibrating when ascending or descending
    D. the foot of the ladder from slipping

20. In construction work, practically all accidents can be blamed on the   20._____
    A. failure of an individual to give close attention to the job assigned to him
    B. use of improper tools
    C. lack of cooperation among the men in a gang
    D. fact that an incompetent man was placed in a key position

21. If it is necessary for you to do some work with your hands under a piece of heavy equip-   21._____
    ment while a fellow worker lifts up and holds one end of it by means of a pinch bar, one
    important precaution you should take is to

    A. wear gloves
    B. watch the bar to be ready if it slips
    C. insert a temporary block to support the piece
    D. work as fast as possible

22. Employees of the transit system whose work requires them to enter upon the tracks in   22._____
    the subway are cautioned not to wear loose fitting clothing.
    The MOST important reason for this caution is that loose fitting clothing may

    A. interfere when men are using heavy tools
    B. catch on some projection of a passing train
    C. tear more easily than snug fitting clothing
    D. give insufficient protection against subway dust

23. The MOST important reason for insisting on neatness in maintenance quarters is that it   23._____

    A. keeps the men busy in slack periods
    B. prevents tools from becoming rusty
    C. makes a good impression on visitors and officials
    D. decreases the chances of accidents to employees

24. Maintenance workers whose duties require them to do certain types of work generally   24._____
    work in pairs.
    The LEAST likely of the following possible reasons for this practice is that

    A. some of the work requires two men
    B. the men can help each other in case of accident
    C. there is too much equipment for one man to carry
    D. it protects against vandalism

25. A foreman reprimands a helper for actions in violation of the rules and regulations.   25._____
    The BEST reaction of the helper in this situation is to

    A. tell the foreman that he was careful and that he did not take any chances
    B. explain that he took this action to save time
    C. keep quiet and accept the criticism
    D. demand that the foreman show him the rule he violated

KEY (CORRECT ANSWERS)

1.	A	11.	C
2.	D	12.	B
3.	D	13.	C
4.	D	14.	D
5.	A	15.	A
6.	C	16.	B
7.	C	17.	C
8.	C	18.	B
9.	A	19.	D
10.	A	20.	A

21. C
22. B
23. D
24. D
25. C

ARITHMETICAL REASONING
EXAMINATION SECTION
TEST 1

DIRECTIONS: Each question or incomplete statement is followed by several suggested answers or completions. Select the one that BEST answers the question or completes the statement. *PRINT THE LETTER OF THE CORRECT ANSWER IN THE SPACE AT THE RIGHT.*

1. A supplier quotes a list price of $172.00 less 15 and 10 percent for twelve tools. The actual cost for these twelve tools is MOST NEARLY 1.____

   A. $146   B. $132   C. $129   D. $112

2. If the diameter of a circular piece of sheet metal is 1 1/2 feet, the area, in square inches, is MOST NEARLY 2.____

   A. 1.77   B. 2.36   C. 254   D. 324

3. The sum of 5'6", 7'3", 9'3 1/2", and 3'7 1/4" is 3.____

   A. 19'8 1/2"   B. 22' 1/2"   C. 25'7 3/4"   D. 28'8 3/4"

4. If the floor area of one shop is 15' by 21'3" and the size of an adjacent shop is 18' by 30'6", then the TOTAL floor area of these two shops is _____ square feet. 4.____

   A. 1127.75   B. 867.75   C. 549.0   D. 318.75

5. The fraction which is equal to 0.875 is 5.____

   A. 7/16   B. 5/8   C. 3/4   D. 7/8

6. The sum of 1/2, 2 1/32, 4 3/16, and 1 7/8 is MOST NEARLY 6.____

   A. 9.593   B. 9.625   C. 9.687   D. 10.593

7. If the base of a right triangle is 9" and the altitude is 12", the length of the third side will be 7.____

   A. 13"   B. 14"   C. 15"   D. 16"

8. If a steel bar 1" in diameter and 12' long weighs 32 lbs., then the weight of a piece of this bar 5'9" long is MOST NEARLY _____ lbs. 8.____

   A. 15.33   B. 15.26   C. 16.33   D. 15.06

9. The diameter of a circle whose circumference is 12" is MOST NEARLY 9.____

   A. 3.82"   B. 3.72"   C. 3.62"   D. 3.52"

10. A dimension of 39/64 inches converted to decimals is MOST NEARLY 10.____

    A. .600"   B. .609"   C. .607"   D. .611"

11. A farm worker was paid a weekly wage of $415.20 for a 44-hour work week. As a result of a new labor contract, he is paid $431.40 a week for a 40-hour work week with time and one-half pay for time worked in excess of 40 hours in any work week.
    If he continues to work 44 hours weekly under the new contract, the amount by which his average hourly rate for a 44-hour work week under the new contract exceeds the hourly rate previously paid him lies between _____ and _____, inclusive.

    A. 80¢; $1.00   B. $1.00; $1.20
    C. $1.25; $1.45   D. $1.50; $1.70

12. The sum of 4 feet 3 1/4 inches, 7 feet 2 1/2 inches, and 11 feet 1/4 inch is _____ feet _____ inches.

    A. 21; 6 1/4   B. 22; 6   C. 23; 5   D. 24; 5 3/4

13. The number 0.038 is read as

    A. 38 tenths   B. 38 hundredths
    C. 38 thousandths   D. 38 ten-thousandths

14. Assume that an employee is paid at the rate of $10.86 per hour with time and a half for overtime past 40 hours in a week.
    If he works 43 hours in a week, his gross weekly pay is

    A. $434.40   B. $438.40   C. $459.18   D. $483.27

15. The sum of the following dimensions: 3'2 1/4", 8 7/8", 2'6 3/8", 2'9 3/4", and 1'0" is

    A. 16'7 1/4"   B. 10'7 1/4"   C. 10'3 1/4"   D. 9'3 1/4"

16. Two gears are meshed together and have a gear ratio of 6 to 1.
    If the small gear rotates 120 revolutions per minute, the large gear rotates at

    A. 20   B. 40   C. 60   D. 720

17. The vacuum side of a compound gage reads 14 inches of vacuum. The barometer reading is 29.76 inches of mercury. The equivalent absolute pressure of the compound gage reading, in inches of mercury, is MOST likely

    A. 15.06   B. 15.76   C. 43.06   D. 43.76

18. The fraction 5/8 expressed as a decimal is

    A. 0.125   B. 0.412   C. 0.625   D. 0.875

19. If 300 feet of a certain size pipe weighs 450 pounds, the number of pounds that 100 feet will weigh is

    A. 1,350   B. 150   C. 300   D. 250

20. As an oiler, you work for a facility that has automobiles that use, on the average, 600 quarts of one grade of lubricating oil every month.
    The number of one-gallon cans of the above oil that should be ordered each month to meet this requirement is

    A. 100   B. 125   C. 140   D. 150

21. The inside dimensions of a rectangular oil gravity tank are: height 15", width 9", length 10".
    The amount of oil in the tank, in gallons, (231 cu.in. = 1 gallon), when the oil level is 9" high, is MOST NEARLY

    A. 2.3   B. 3.5   C. 5.2   D. 5.8

22. If 30 gallons of oil cost $76.80, 45 gallons of oil at the same rate will cost

    A. $91.20   B. $115.20   C. $123.20   D. $131.20

23. If an oiler earns $18,000 in the first six months of a year and receives a 10% raise in salary for the next six months of the same year, his TOTAL earnings for the year will be

    A. $36,000   B. $37,500   C. $37,800   D. $39,600

24. If the cost of lubricating oil increases 15%, then a gallon of oil which used to cost $10.00 will now cost MOST NEARLY

    A. $10.50   B. $11.00   C. $11.50   D. $12.00

25. The sum of 7/8", 3/4", 1/2", and 3/8" is

    A. 2 1/8"   B. 2 1/4"   C. 2 3/8"   D. 2 1/2"

KEY (CORRECT ANSWERS)

1. B
2. C
3. C
4. B
5. D

6. A
7. C
8. A
9. A
10. B

11. A
12. B
13. C
14. D
15. C

16. A
17. B
18. C
19. B
20. D

21. B
22. B
23. C
24. C
25. D

SOLUTIONS TO PROBLEMS

1. Actual cost = ($172)(.85)(.90) = $131.58 ≈ $132

2. Radius = .75', then area = (3.14)(.75)^2 ≈ 1.77 sq.ft.
   Since 1 sq.ft. = 144 sq.in., the area ≈ 254 sq.in.

3. 5'6" + 7'3" + 9'3 1/2" + 3'7 1/4" = 24'19 3/4" = 25'7 3/4"

4. Total area = (15)(21.25) + (18)(30.5) = 867.75 sq.ft.

5. .875 = 875/1000 = 7/8

6. 1 1/2 + 2 1/32 + 4 3/16 + 1 7/8 = 8 51/32 = 9 19/32 = 9.593

7. Third side = $\sqrt{9^2+12^2} = \sqrt{225} = 15"$

8. Let x = weight. Then, 12/32 = 5.75/x. Solving, x ≈ 15.33 lbs.

9. 12" = (3.14)(diameter), so diameter ≈ 3.82"

10. $\frac{39}{64}$" = .609375" ≈ .609"

11. Under his new contract, the weekly wage for 44 hours can be found by first determining his hourly rate for the first 40 hours = $431.40 ÷ 40 ≈ $10.80. Now, his time and one-half pay will = ($10.80)(1.5) = $16.20. His weekly wage for the new contract = $431.40 + (4)($16.20) = $496.20. His new hourly rate for 44 hours = $496.20 ÷ 44 ≈ $10.34. Under the old contract, his hourly rate for 44 hours was $415.20 ÷ 44 = $9.44. His hourly rate increase = $10.34 - $9.44 = $0.90. (Answer key: between $0.80 and $1.00)

12. 4'3 1/4" + 7'2 1/2" + 11' 1/4" = 22'6"

13. .038 = 38 thousandths

14. ($10.86)(40) + ($16.29)(3) = $483.27

15. 3'2 1/4" + 8 7/8" + 2'6 3/8" + 2'9 3/4" + 1'0" = 8'25 18/8" = 10'3 1/4"

16. The gear ratio is inversely proportional to the gear size. Let x = large gear's rpm. Then, 6/1 = 120/x. Solving, x = 20

17. Subtract 14 from 29.76

18. 5/8 = .625

19. Let x = number of pounds. Then, 300/450 = 100/x. Solving, x = 150

20. 600 quarts = 150 gallons, since 4 quarts = 1 gallon

21. (9")(9")(10") = 810 cu.in. Then, 810 ÷ 231 ≈ 3.5

22. Let x = unknown cost. Then, 30/$76.80 = 45/x. Solving, x = $115.20

23. $18,000 + ($18,000)(1.10) = $37,800

24. ($10.00)(1.15) = $11.50

25. 7/8" + 3/4" + 1/2" + 3/8" = 20/8" = 2 1/2"

TEST 2

DIRECTIONS: Each question or incomplete statement is followed by several suggested answers or completions. Select the one that BEST answers the question or completes the statement. *PRINT THE LETTER OF THE CORRECT ANSWER IN THE SPACE AT THE RIGHT.*

1. A sheet metal plate has been cut in the form of a right triangle with sides of 5, 12, and 13 inches.
   The area of this plate, in square inches, is

   A. 30   B. 32 1/2   C. 60   D. 78

   1.___

2. If steel weighs 480 lbs. per cubic foot, the weight of an 18" x 18" x 2" steel base plate is _____ lbs.

   A. 180   B. 216   C. 427   D. 648

   2.___

3. By trial, it is found that by using 2 cubic feet of sand, a 5 cubic foot batch of concrete is produced.
   Using the same proportions, the amount of sand, in cubic feet, required to produce 2 cubic yards of concrete is MOST NEARLY

   A. 7   B. 22   C. 27   D. 45

   3.___

4. The total number of cubic yards of earth to be removed to make a trench 3'9" wide, 25'0" long, and 4'3" deep is MOST NEARLY

   A. 53.1   B. 35.4   C. 26.6   D. 14.8

   4.___

5. A large number of 2 x 4 studs, some 10'5" long and some 6'5 1/2" long, are required for a job.
   To minimize waste, it would be PREFERABLE to order lengths of _____ feet.

   A. 16   B. 17   C. 18   D. 19

   5.___

6. A 6" pipe is connected to a 4" pipe through a reducer. If 100 cubic feet of water is flowing through the 6" pipe per minute, the flow, in cubic feet, per minute through the 4" pipe is

   A. 225   B. 100   C. 66.6   D. 44.4

   6.___

7. If steel weighs 0.28 pounds per cubic inch, then the weight, in pounds, of a 2" square steel bar 120" long is MOST NEARLY

   A. 115   B. 125   C. 135   D. 155

   7.___

8. A three-inch diameter steel bar two feet long weighs MOST NEARLY (assume steel weighs 480 lbs./cu.ft.) _____ lbs.

   A. 48   B. 58   C. 68   D. 78

   8.___

9. The area of a circular plate will be reduced by 5% if a sector removed from it has an angle of _____ degrees.

   A. 18   B. 24   C. 32   D. 60

   9.___

10. If a 4 1/16 inch shaft wears six thousandths of an inch, the NEW diameter will be _____ inches.

   A. 4.0031   B. 4.0565   C. 4.0578   D. 4.0605

11. A set of mechanical plan drawings is drawn to a scale of 1/8" = 1 foot.
   If a length of pipe measures 15 7/16" on the drawing, the ACTUAL length of the pipe is _____ feet.

   A. 121.5   B. 122.5   C. 123.5   D. 124.5

12. An electrical drawing is drawn to a scale of 1/4" = 1'. If a length of conduit on the drawing measures 7 3/8", the actual length of the conduit, in feet, is

   A. 7.5   B. 15.5   C. 22.5   D. 29.5

13. Assume that you have assigned 6 mechanics to do a job that must be finished in 4 days. At the end of 3 days, your men have completed only two-thirds of the job. In order to complete the job on time and because the job is such that it cannot be speeded up, you should assign a MINIMUM of _____ extra men.

   A. 3   B. 4   C. 5   D. 6

14. Assume that a trench is 42" wide, 5' deep, and 100' long. If the unit price of excavating the trench is $105 per cubic yard, the cost of excavating the trench is MOST NEARLY

   A. $6,805   B. $15,330   C. $21,000   D. $63,000

15. If the scale on a shop drawing is 1/4 inch to the foot, then the length of a part which measures 2 3/8 inches long on the drawing is ACTUALLY _____ feet.

   A. 9 1/2   B. 8 1/2   C. 7 1/4   D. 4 1/4

16. It is necessary to pour a new concrete floor for a shop. If the dimensions of the concrete slab for the floor are to be 27' x 18' x 6", then the number of cubic yards of concrete that must be poured is

   A. 9   B. 16   C. 54   D. 243

17. The jaws of a vise move 1/4" for each complete turn of the handle.
   The number of complete turns necessary to open the jaws 2 3/4" is

   A. 9   B. 10   C. 11   D. 12

18. Assume that a jobbing shop is to submit a price for a contract involving 300 pieces of work. Assume that material costs 50 cents per piece, labor costs $7.50 an hour, and a lathe operator can complete 5 pieces in an hour.
   If overhead is 40% of material and labor costs and the profit is 10% of all costs, the submitted price for the entire job will be

   A. $630.24   B. $872.80   C. $900.00   D. $924.00

19. The following formula is used in connection with the three-wire method of measuring pitch diameters of screw threads: $G = \dfrac{0.57735}{N}$, where G = wire size and N = number of threads per inch.
According to this formula, the proper size of wire for a 1"-8NC thread is MOST NEARLY

    A. .0722"   B. .7217"   C. .0072"   D. .0074"

20. A millimeter is 1/25.4 of an inch and there are 10 millimeters to a centimeter. If a piece of stock measures 127 centimeters long, the length of the stock, in feet and inches, would be MOST NEARLY

    A. 2'1"   B. 4'2"   C. 8'4"   D. 41'8"

21. For a certain job, you will need 25 steel bars 1 inch in diameter and 4"6" long. If these bars weigh 3 pounds per foot of length, then the TOTAL weight for all 25 bars is _____ pounds.

    A. 13.5   B. 75.0   C. 112.5   D. 337.5

22. If steel weighs 0.30 pounds per cubic inch, then the weight of a 2 inch square steel bar 90 inches long is _____ pounds.

    A. 27   B. 54   C. 108   D. 360

23. A concrete wall is 36' long, 9' high, and 1 1/2' thick. The number of cubic yards of concrete that were needed to make this wall is

    A. 14   B. 18   C. 27   D. 36

24. If the scale on a shop drawing is 1/2 inch to the foot, then the length of a part which measures 41/4 inches long on the drawing has a length of APPROXIMATELY _____ feet.

    A. 2 1/8   B. 4 1/4   C. 8 1/2   D. 10 3/4

25. If the allowable load on a wooden scaffold is 60 pounds per square foot and the scaffold surface area is 3 feet by 12 feet, then the MAXIMUM total distributed load that is permitted on the scaffold is _____ pounds.

    A. 720   B. 1,800   C. 2,160   D. 2,400

KEY (CORRECT ANSWERS)

1. A
2. A
3. B
4. D
5. B

6. B
7. C
8. A
9. A
10. B

11. C
12. D
13. A
14. A
15. A

16. A
17. C
18. D
19. A
20. B

21. D
22. C
23. B
24. C
25. C

SOLUTIONS TO PROBLEMS

1. Area = (1/2)(base)(height) = (1/2)(5")(12") = 30 sq.in.

2. Volume = (18") (18") (2") = 648 cu.in. = 648/1720 cu.ft.
   Then, (480)(648/1720) = $\approx$ 180 lbs.

3. 2 cu.yds. = 54 cu.ft. Let x = required cubic feet of sand. Then, 2/5 = x/54. Solving, x = 21.6 (or about 22)

4. (3.75')(25')(4.25') = 398.4375 cu.ft. $\approx$ 14.8 cu.yds.

5. 10'5" + 6'5 1/2" = 16'10 1/2", so lengths of 17 feet are needed

6. The amount of water flowing through each pipe must be equal.

7. (2")(2")(120") = 480 cu. in. Then, (480)(.28) $\approx$ 135 lbs.

8. Volume = (π) (.125 ')^2 (2) $\approx$ .1 cu.ft. Then, (.1)(480) = 48 lbs.

9. (360°)(.05) - 18°

10. 4 1/16 - .006 = 4.0625 - .006 = 4.0565

11. 15 7/16" $\div$ 1/8" = 247/16 . 8/1 = 123.5. Then, (123.5)(1 ft.) = 123.5 ft.

12. 7 3/8" $\div$ 1/4" = 59/8 . 4/1 = 29.5 Then, (29.5)(1 ft.) = 29.5 ft.

13. (6)(4) = 24 man-days normally required. Since after 3 days only the equivalent of (2/3)(24) = 16 man-days of work has been 1 done, 8 man-days of work is still left. 16 $\div$ 3 = 5 1/3, which means the crew is equivalent to only 5 1/3 men. To do the 8 man-days of work, it will require at least 8 - 5 1/3 = 2 2/3 = 3 additional men.

14. (3.5')(5')(100') = 1750 cu.ft. $\approx$ 64.8 cu.yds. Then, (64.8)($105) $\approx$ $6805

15. 2 3/8" $\div$ 1/4" = 19/8 . 4/1 = 9 1/2 Then, (9 1/2)(1 ft.) = 9 1/2 feet

16. (27')(18')(1/2') = 243 cu.ft. = 9 cu.yds. (1 cu.yd. = 27 cu.ft.)

17. 2 3/4" $\div$ 1/4" = 11/4 . 4/1 = 11

18. Material cost = (300)($.50) = $150. Labor cost = ($7.50)(300/5) = $450. Overhead = (.40)($150+$450) = $240. Profit = .10($150+$450+$240) = $84. Submitted price = $150 + $450 + $240 + $84 = $924

19. 6 = .57735" $\div$ 8 = .0722"

20. 127 cm = 1270 mm = 1270/25.4" ≈ 50" = 4.2"

21. (25)(4.5') = 112.5' Then, (112.5X3) = 337.5 lbs.

22. (2")(2")(90") = 360 cu.in. Then, (360)(30) = 108 lbs.

23. (36')(9')(1 1/2') = 486 cu.ft. = 18 cu.yds. (1 cu.yd. = 27 cu.ft.)

24. 4 1/4" ÷ 1/2" = 17/4 . 2/1 = 8 1/2. Then, (8 1/2)(1 ft.) = 8 1/2 ft.

25. (12')(3') = 36 sq.ft. Then, (36)(60) = 2160 lbs.

TEST 3

DIRECTIONS: Each question or incomplete statement is followed by several suggested answers or completions. Select the one that BEST answers the question or completes the statement. *PRINT THE LETTER OF THE CORRECT ANSWER IN THE SPACE AT THE RIGHT.*

1. A right triangular metal sheet for a roofing job has sides of 36 inches and 4 feet. The length of the remaining side is

    A. 7 feet
    B. 6 feet
    C. 60 inches
    D. 90 inches

    1.___

2. A U.S. Standard Gauge thickness is given as 0.15625. This thickness, in fractions of an inch, is MOST NEARLY _____ inches.

    A. 1/8 B. 4/32 C. 5/32 D. 3/64

    2.___

3. The weight per 100 of sheet metal fasteners is given as 2/3 pound. The APPROXIMATE number of fasteners in a 2-pound package is

    A. 166 B. 200 C. 300 D. 266

    3.___

4. The decimal equivalent of 27/32 is MOST NEARLY

    A. 0.813 B. 0.828 C. 0.844 D. 0.859

    4.___

5. If a scaled measurement of 1'3" on the drawing of a sheet metal layout represents an actual length of 10'0", then the drawing has been made to a scale of _____ inch to the foot.

    A. 3/4 B. 1 1/4 C. 1 1/2 D. 1 3/4

    5.___

6. Two and two-thirds tees can be made from one sheet of steel. If 24 tees must be made, then the number of sheets required is

    A. 6 B. 7 C. 8 D. 9

    6.___

7. A main duct 20 inches in diameter discharges into two branch ducts. The sum of the areas of the branches is to be equal to the area of the main duct. One branch is 12 inches in diameter. The diameter of the other branch is _____ inches.

    A. 16 B. 12 C. 10 D. 8

    7.___

8. If steel weighs 480 lbs. per cubic foot, the weight of 10 sheets, each 6 feet by 3 feet by 1/32 inch, is _____ lbs.

    A. 2,700 B. 1,237 C. 270 D. 225

    8.___

9. The area, in square inches, of a right triangle that has sides of 12 1/2, 10, and 7 1/2 inches is

    A. 18 1/4 B. 37 1/2 C. 75 D. 60

    9.___

10. In making a container to hold 1 gallon (231 cu.in.) and to be 6 inches in diameter at the top and 8 inches in diameter at the bottom, the height must be, in inches,

    A. 10.0   B. 8.2   C. 4.6   D. 6

11. A sheet metal worker is given a job to make a transition piece from a 8 1/2" diameter duct to an 11 1/4" diameter duct. If the length of the transition piece is 5 1/2" for each inch change in diameter, then the length of the transition piece is

    A. 14 7/8"   B. 15"   C. 15 1/8"   D. 15 1/4"

12. A duct layout is drawn to a scale of 3/8" to a foot. If the length of a run shown on the drawing scales 7 1/2", then the ACTUAL length of the run is

    A. 19'6"   B. 19'9"   C. 20'0"   D. 20'3"

13. An 18" x 24" duct is to be connected to a 24" x 24" duct by means of an eccentric transition piece (3 sides flush). If the taper is to be 1" in 4", then the length of the transition piece is

    A. 6"   B. 12"   C. 18"   D. 24"

14. Twenty-seven pairs of 3/8" diameter rods each 3'3 1/2" long are needed to support a duct.
    If the available rods are ten feet long, then the MINIMUM number of rods that will be needed to make the twenty-seven sets is

    A. 9   B. 12   C. 15   D. 18

15. A rectangular sheet metal air duct with open ends is 12 feet long and 15" x 20" in cross-section. If one square foot of the sheet metal weighs 1/2 pound, then the TOTAL weight of the duct is _____ lbs.

    A. 10   B. 17 1/2   C. 35   D. 150

16. The sum of 1/12 and 1/4 is

    A. 1/3   B. 5/12   C. 7/12   D. 3/8

17. The product of 12 and 2 1/3 is

    A. 27   B. 28   C. 29   D. 30

18. If 4 1/2 is subtracted from 7 1/5, the remainder is

    A. 3 7/10   B. 2 7/10   C. 3 3/10   D. 2 3/10

19. The number of cubic yards in 47 cubic feet is MOST NEARLY

    A. 1.70   B. 1.74   C. 1.78   D. 1.82

20. A wall 8'0" high by 12'6" long has a window opening 4'0" high by 3'6" wide. The net area of the wall (allowing for the window opening) is, in square feet,

    A. 86   B. 87   C. 88   D. 89

21. A worker's hourly rate is $11.36.   21.____
    If he works 11 1/2 hours, he should receive

    A. $129.84   B. $130.64   C. $131.48   D. $132.24

22. The number of cubic feet in 3 cubic yards is   22.____

    A. 81   B. 82   C. 83   D. 84

23. At an annual rate of $.40 per $100, what is the fire insurance premium for one year on a   23.____
    house that is insured for $80,000?

    A. $120   B. $160   C. $240   D. $320

24. A meter equals approximately 1.09 yards.   24.____
    How much longer, in yards, is a 100-meter dash than a 100-yard dash?

    A. 6   B. 8   C. 9   D. 12

25. A train leaves New York City at 8:10 A.M. and arrives in Buffalo at 4:45 P.M. on the same   25.____
    day. How long, in hours and minutes, does it take the train to make the trip?
    _____ hours, _____ minutes.

    A. 6; 22   B. 7; 16   C. 7; 28   D. 8; 35

KEY (CORRECT ANSWERS)

1. C	11. C
2. C	12. C
3. C	13. D
4. C	14. D
5. C	15. C
6. D	16. A
7. A	17. B
8. D	18. B
9. B	19. B
10. D	20. A

21. B
22. A
23. D
24. C
25. D

SOLUTIONS TO PROBLEMS

1. Let x = remaining side. Converting to inches, $x^2 = 36^2 + 48^2$ So, $x^2 = 3600$. Solving, $x = 60$ inches.

2. $.15625 = \dfrac{15{,}625}{100{,}000} = \dfrac{5}{32}$

3. $2 \div 2/3 = 3$. Then, $(3)(100) = 300$ fasteners

4. $27/32 = .84375 \approx .844$

5. 1'3" ÷ 10 = 15" ÷ 10 = 1 1/2"

6. $24 \div 2\,2/3 = 24/1 . 3/8 = 9$

7. Area of main duct = $(\pi)(10^2) = 100\pi$. One of the branches has an area of $(\pi)(6^2) = 36\pi$. Thus, the area of the 2nd branch = $100\pi - 36\pi = 64\pi$. The 2nd branch's radius must be 8" and its diameter must be 16".

8. Volume = (1/384')(6')(3') = .046875 cu.ft. Then, 10 sheets have a volume of .46875 cu.ft. Now, (.46875)(480) = 225 lbs.

9. Note that $(7\,1/2)^2 + (10)^2 = (12\,1/2)^2$, so that this is a right triangle. Area = (1/2)(10")(7 1/2") = 37 1/2 sq.in.

10. $231 = \dfrac{h}{3}[(\pi)(3)^2 + (\pi)(4)^2 + \sqrt{(9\pi)(16\pi)}]$, where h = required height. Then,

    $231 = \dfrac{h}{3}(9\pi + 16\pi + 12\pi)$. Simplifying, $231 = 37\pi h/3$.
    Solving, h ~ 5.96" or 6"

11. 11 1/4 - 8 1/2 = 2 3/4. Then, (2 3/4)(5 1/2) = 11/4 . 11/2 = 15 1/8

12. 7 1/2" ÷ 3/8" = 15/2 . 8/3 = 20 Then, (20)(1 ft.) = 20 feet

13. 24" - 18" = 6" Then, (6")(4) = 24"

14. 3'3 1/2" = 39.5". Now, (27)(2)(39.5") = 2133". 10 ft. = 120". Finally, 2133 ÷ 120 = 17.775, so 18 rods are needed.

15. Surface area = (2)(12')(1 1/4') + (2)(12')(1 2/3') = 70 sq.ft. Then, (70)(1/2 lb.) - 35 lbs.

16. 1/12 + 1/4 = 4/12 = 1/3

17. (12)(2 1/3) = 12/1 . 7/3 = 28

18. 7 1/5 - 4 1/2 = 7 2/10 - 4 5/10 = 6 12/10 - 4 5/10 = 2 7/10

19. 47 cu.ft. = 47/27 cu.yds. = 1.74 cu.yds.

20. (8')(12.5') - (4')(3.5') = 86 sq.ft.

21. ($11.36)(11.5) = $130.64

22. 1 cu.yd. = 27 cu.ft., so 3 cu.yds. = 81 cu.ft.

23. $80,000 ÷ $100 = 800. Then, (800)($.40) = $320

24. 100 meters = 109 yds. Then, 109 - 100 = 9 yds.

25. 4:45 P.M. - 8:10 AM. = 8 hrs. 35 min.

www.ingramcontent.com/pod-product-compliance
Lightning Source LLC
Chambersburg PA
CBHW081826300426
44116CB00014B/2494